What people are saying about ...

THE MARRIAGE GAME PLAN

"On the wedding day, what couple does not want to have a successful marriage? Yet we know that all too often, after the ceremony these dreams begin to fade. George and Tondra can identify with that reality. In this book, they share their struggles and the lessons they have learned about how to have a successful marriage. They share not only the game plan but how to implement the plan. This book will be extremely helpful for any couple who wants to make their marital dreams come true."

Gary Chapman, PhD, bestselling author of *The 5 Love Languages*

"Great marriages are built on healthy values, personal character, and the right tools. Unfortunately, many couples are without one or more of these aspects, and the results are all too often emotional disconnection, loneliness, and a sense of helplessness. The Gregorys have provided all three of these essentials in a warm and engaging manner. You'll learn a biblical model of what a marriage is, how to be the best mate you can be, and what tools you can employ. The authors' personal vulnerability and humor makes this a read to look forward to. And the questions and action steps section after each chapter makes it a truly permanent resource to refresh your connection. Highly recommended!"

John Townsend, PhD, psychologist and author of the *New York Times*–bestselling *Boundaries* book series, founder of Townsend Institute of Leadership and Counseling at Concordia University Irvine and the Townsend Leadership Program

"*The Marriage Game Plan* is your playbook for a winning marriage. On every page, George and Tondra coach you through practical, game-changing strategies for a strong and lasting relationship. Whether you're in the early quarter or the final plays, this book is for you."

Drs. Les and Leslie Parrott, #1 *New York Times*–bestselling authors of *Saving Your Marriage Before It Starts*

"We have known Pastor George and Tondra since they came to the Los Angeles Chargers to serve as our chaplain. It's a position that George still holds to this day. The NFL is riddled with hurdles and hardships for couples who often don't have anywhere to turn for sound biblical guidance. The insular nature of this job and the unique set of adversities can make it hard for others to relate to our struggles. But the Gregorys were always there to provide guidance and prayer rooted in the Word. We are a testament to this because my wife and I have both had to seek prayer and guidance from them during this NFL journey. *The Marriage Game Plan* provides couples with biblically based tools to keep their marriages intact by putting God first and seeing His hand in everything. Their faithfulness and wisdom as a godly couple will undoubtedly be a blessing to everyone who reads this book."

Anthony Lynn, former NFL head coach of the Los Angeles Chargers (2017–2021)

"Working in football, I could not imagine going through an entire week of practice and not having a game plan for success when it came time to face the opponent! *The Marriage Game Plan* is a must-read for couples who are starting their life's journey, are in the middle of their journey, or are reflecting on their journey together. George and Tondra share from their personal experiences and heartfelt ministry to help others in navigating marriage through establishing trust as teammates, overcoming turbulent waters, tackling tough conversations, and celebrating victories along the way. This is a must-read to establish your marriage game plan to be ready for *game day*—each and every day!"

Arthur Hightower, senior director of player engagement, Los Angeles Chargers

"As a couple navigating the whirlwind of the NFL, having mentors who truly understand the demands of both marriage and a high-profile lifestyle has been invaluable to us. This incredible couple has offered guidance that feels both personal and practical. They have a gift for meeting couples right where they are, understanding their unique challenges, and providing the tools necessary to cultivate a relationship built on trust, love, and shared vision. In *The Marriage Game Plan*, the way the Gregorys compare the journey of marriage to the dynamics of a winning team resonated deeply with us—seeing our relationship as a partnership where both of us are on the same side, playing for the same goal. From tackling tough conversations to celebrating victories, this book offers practical, compassionate guidance that will inspire you to not just survive marriage but thrive in it. It's a beautiful reminder that with the right tools, teamwork, and heart, marriage can truly be one of life's greatest victories."

Demario and Tamela Davis, All-Pro linebacker for the New Orleans Saints, certified life coach, blogger, podcast host

"This is an outstanding outline for couples to abide by, whether newlywed or together for more than forty years, for longevity in their relationship. As you begin to delve into the chapters of *The Marriage Game Plan*, you will start to understand how to repair relationships and make your marriage a success. This is an inspiring read that will stimulate your marriage by providing activities and questions to give you a great plan for marital stability. George and Tondra's mission to write this book has created a resource for successful marriages that will give you insight on how to avoid the pitfalls you may encounter as you navigate life as a couple."

George Stewart, VP of Game Day/Operations, NFL

"In *The Marriage Game Plan*, George and Tondra draw upon personal experiences from their dating life and marriage to encourage and challenge couples to put together a plan that can withstand the ups and downs of a relationship—a championship-caliber plan that will expose the enemy of marriage and create clarity for the purpose of your union with your spouse. This book will help you understand what it means to have Christ at the head of your marriage."

Leslie Frazier, assistant head coach of the Seattle Seahawks

"George and Tondra's marriage testimony is truly powerful! In *The Marriage Game Plan*, they generously unpack thirty years of wisdom, offering thoughtful and practical steps to build a marriage that lasts. Our marriage has been deeply impacted by their guidance and friendship. The principles in this book can help you maintain, restore, rebuild, and renew your relationship while living out your purpose. We are grateful that other couples will also have the opportunity to benefit from their experience."

Kevin and Bebe Nickerson, founder of GameBreakers Academy, official chaplains of the Los Angeles Rams (Super Bowl LVI champions)

"One thing you'll consistently find among extraordinarily successful people is they have coaches! Over the years, we've had a front-row seat to witness George and Tondra guide countless couples to achieve the most fulfilling days of their marriages. In *The Marriage Game Plan*, they offer a master class filled with the proven strategies and practical wisdom that every couple needs to create a thriving, joyful, and lasting marriage. Whether you're looking to reignite the spark, strengthen your connection, or overcome challenges, George and Tondra will equip you with the tools to succeed in your own marriage journey."

Clayton and Ashlee Hurst, marriage pastors at Lakewood Church, authors of *Hope for Your Marriage*

"Fewer people are getting married, and when they do marry, they're older, and then divorce is at an all-time high. Why? Well, as it has been said, when people fail to plan, they plan to fail. George is a dear friend, and I deeply respect both him and the way he and Tondra have committed to walking people into the joy that God designed marriage to be. The world needs this book."

Joshua Broome, speaker and author of *7 Lies That Will Ruin Your Life*

"George and Tondra Gregory have committed their lives and ministry to helping couples thrive in their marriages. Among the several tools and books about marriage out there, *The Marriage Game Plan* is the most accessible and offers practical tools that can immediately improve communication between couples and help them co-create a vision for their marriage. Using wit, humor, and their own life story, they effectively bring hard and timeless truths to life and guide couples in deepening their marriage and love for each other. They debunk stereotypes about the roles of wives and husbands that swirl in Christian communities to align marriage with biblical principles. *The Marriage Game Plan* is an effective tool for marriages at any stage—from newly married to those who are celebrating decades of anniversaries—and can be studied and re-studied over the course of married life."

Nancy E. Hill, PhD, developmental psychologist, the Charles Bigelow Professor of Education at Harvard University, author of *The End of Adolescence*

GEORGE AND TONDRA GREGORY

The Marriage GAME PLAN

DEVELOPING A WINNING STRATEGY FOR MARITAL SUCCESS

THE MARRIAGE GAME PLAN
Published by David C Cook
4050 Lee Vance Drive
Colorado Springs, CO 80918 U.S.A.

Integrity Music Limited, a Division of David C Cook
Brighton, East Sussex BN1 2RE, England

DAVID C COOK® and related marks are registered trademarks of David C Cook.

All rights reserved. Except for brief excerpts for review purposes,
no part of this book may be reproduced or used in any form
without written permission from the publisher.

The website addresses recommended throughout this book are offered as a resource to you. These websites are not intended in any way to be or imply an endorsement on the part of David C Cook, nor do we vouch for their content.

Details in some stories have been changed to protect the identities of the persons involved.

Unless otherwise noted, all Scripture quotations are taken from the Holy Bible, New International Version®, NIV®. Copyright © 1973, 2011 by Biblica, Inc.™ Used by permission of Zondervan. All rights reserved worldwide. www.zondervan.com. The "NIV" and "New International Version" are trademarks registered in the United States Patent and Trademark Office by Biblica, Inc.™ Scripture quotations marked ESV are taken from the ESV® Bible (The Holy Bible, English Standard Version®), copyright © 2001 by Crossway, a publishing ministry of Good News Publishers. Used by permission. All rights reserved; NKJV are taken from the New King James Version®. Copyright © 1982 by Thomas Nelson. Used by permission. All rights reserved; NLT are taken from the Holy Bible, New Living Translation, copyright © 1996, 2015 by Tyndale House Foundation. Used by permission of Tyndale House Publishers, Carol Stream, Illinois 60188. All rights reserved.

Library of Congress Control Number 2024943838
ISBN 978-0-8307-8674-9
eISBN 978-0-8307-8675-6

© 2025 George Gregory and Latondra Gregory

The Team: Susan McPherson, Stephanie Bennett, Marianne Hering, Judy Gillispie, Karissa Silvers, James Hershberger, Susan Murdock
Cover Design: Micah Kandros
Cover Photo: Andrew James Abajian

Printed in the United States of America
First Edition 2025

1 2 3 4 5 6 7 8 9 10

I dedicate this book to my father (1946–2020) and mother, Henry and Coleen, who modeled a godly marriage for fifty-two years.
—*George*

I dedicate this book to my mom, Shirley, who gave her best to make me the woman I am today.
—*Tondra*

To our amazing children, Jaylen and Camryn, who inspire and challenge us to love deeply and leave a godly legacy.

CONTENTS

Foreword	13
Chapter 1: The Importance of a Game Plan	15
Chapter 2: The Playbook on Marriage	33
Chapter 3: Winning the Home Game	49
Chapter 4: We Are on the Same Team	67
Chapter 5: Facing and Overcoming Your Opponents	85
Chapter 6: Trusting Your Teammate	105
Chapter 7: Victory Mondays	129
Chapter 8: Teamwork in Conflict	147
Chapter 9: Tips for Tackling Tough Conversations	169
Chapter 10: Developing Your Marriage Game Plan	187
Conclusion	201
Small Group Guide	203
Acknowledgments	213
Notes	215

FOREWORD

I remember when I first met George and Tondra Gregory at Saddleback Church many years ago. From the outset I could tell they loved each other deeply and had an incredible passion and heart for helping couples build successful relationships and marriages. The Gregorys work beautifully as a husband-and-wife duo who speak and teach together, which is rare in couples ministry. They have spoken at some of the largest Christian churches in America, which has motivated them to write this book to help more couples.

I believe so strongly in their ministry to couples that I invited them to speak one weekend at all of our services at Saddleback Church. The response from our congregation was so positive that the Gregorys were asked to lead the marriage ministry at Saddleback for several years. They taught classes and hosted date nights for couples seeking to strengthen and grow their relationships.

If you've been married or in a serious relationship for any length of time, you know that occasional or ongoing support is essential for a healthy relationship journey. While many aspire to have a thriving relationship, not everyone possesses the skills and knowledge to overcome challenges and make it work. As the author of *The Purpose Driven Life* and a husband of forty-nine wonderful years, I can attest that every marriage and relationship benefits from trusted voices, mentors, guides, and coaches.

George and Tondra Gregory are among the best in the field. They are nationally recognized marriage coaches and instructors who have helped tens of thousands of couples reimagine marriage through a biblical lens and discover what it can become when approached with intention and care. For more than twenty-five years, the Gregorys have been coaching and counseling couples and families through their marriage ministry, Journey for Life. They offer digital content, classes, retreats, conferences, and group and one-on-one sessions to help couples build stronger, healthier marriages. They tirelessly serve everyday couples in communities across the country and beyond.

As marriage and relationship coaches in the NFL, George and Tondra have supported and mentored professional athletes, coaches, and their families for more than fifteen years. Serving as NFL chaplains for the Los Angeles Chargers and supporting other chaplains and teams across the league have equipped the Gregorys with exceptional insight into helping couples develop winning game plans, craft strategic playbooks for optimal marriage performance, and work together as a team to achieve success.

George and Tondra don't just teach and coach on marriage and relationships as theory—they live it. With thirty years of marriage and the successful launch of two children into adulthood, they are living examples of what a healthy marriage looks like. Through their insightful teaching and practical tools, they offer couples actionable strategies that can transform any relationship.

Reading *The Marriage Game Plan* will undoubtedly deepen and strengthen your relationship. This book is an invaluable resource for any couple ready to invest in their relationship and elevate it to the next level. If you are looking for a marriage book with practical examples, tools, couple's activities, and a guide to help you build your unique marriage game plan, look no further.

Rick Warren
Pastor and founder of Saddleback Church

Chapter 1

THE IMPORTANCE OF A GAME PLAN

The key is not the "will to win" ... everybody has that. It is the will to prepare to win that is important.

Coach Bobby Knight

Have you ever considered how your background, family of origin, and past experiences impact your marriage or future marriage? George and I realized how the differences in our upbringings posed challenges in our relationship almost immediately after our wedding day. As innocent kids growing up, we can be oblivious to how the relationships and experiences in our childhoods are molding us and laying the groundwork for future relationships.

Your family background and upbringing shape your very essence—your identity, behavior, expectations, and relational dynamics. By comprehending your family of origin, you can break free from cyclical patterns, habits, and beliefs that are not helpful to your relationship and instead embrace the healthy, beneficial things you want to keep and build on. Understanding your family of origin and its influence on you and your relationship is an essential component of a successful marriage game plan.

GEORGE'S STORY

I grew up in a middle-class home with two loving parents who modeled a healthy marriage. As the youngest of three children, I saw my parents make a consistent effort to raise us kids with good Christian morals and values. I grew up going to church every Sunday, and some Sundays we went twice! My dad was a well-known southern itinerant pastor who proclaimed Christ's salvation and forgiveness of sins to even the most wretched of sinners. I saw thousands of lives impacted through his preaching and ability to make the Scriptures come alive.

> *We were anxiously rolling the dice without a solid game plan and with no clue about what was ahead of us on our marriage journey.*

In many respects, I knew at an early age that I, too, would become a preacher, but that was not my desire or intent at that time. I could sense God's call on my life, but instead of running toward the call, I found myself running in the opposite direction! Like the prodigal son in Jesus' parable, I ran from God both spiritually and emotionally into the arms of whatever drew me in. Although I sang in the choir, I was far from the perfect choirboy. I was only acting the part of a nice Christian boy. I wanted people to think I had it all together, but inside I was torn apart.

Running away from God's love unfortunately opened me up to country singer Johnny Lee's philosophy: "I was lookin' for love in all the wrong places, lookin' for love in too many faces."[1] Without God's unconditional love and acceptance in my heart, I lived a life of promiscuity where I sought love and acceptance from women and relationships. Wrong choice! The first two years of my college life unfortunately led me down a deep, dark road of sex, alcohol, and partying.

My shipwrecked spiritual and emotional life left a wake of poor relationship choices and many brokenhearted women as I tried to find a friend and a lover. They thought I had it all together because they saw only the superficial George that I was projecting. They had no inkling of the pain I was dealing with on the inside.

TONDRA'S STORY

My mother gave birth to me when she was seventeen years old. My father was also a teenager, but he did not want to accept responsibility for his actions. He abandoned my mother and me when she was pregnant. His reason was "It's not mine." My father has denied me my whole life. My mother never married and raised me alone. She was determined to be strong and raise a strong daughter; however, her idea of strength was colored by the dysfunctional men in her life. My mother's father was an alcoholic who drank himself to death, and her boyfriend abandoned her and their child (me!) when she needed him most.

Growing up in these dreary circumstances was difficult. I had a great mother who did the best she could to raise me alone, and I would not be where I am today without her sacrifice and commitment. Thanks, Mom! However, my mother's heart grew bitter and cold throughout the hardships. Her heart was hardened toward men, and she had enormous mistrust for men and people in general. She dealt with her fears through control and criticism. She was determined to protect me from ever being hurt or betrayed by anyone. This control, along with a cloud of shame, abandonment, and rejection, created the perfect storm for a lost, confused girl with little self-worth.

Because I was desperate for freedom and independence, I went off to college looking for the fullness of life, joy, and happiness. Little did I know this pursuit would lead me spiraling into some of the darkest places I could ever imagine. I lived "the high life," or what life appeared to be all about: partying, drinking, using drugs, and being sexually free. I lived life on the edge with a gnarly crowd, which could have landed me in jail or in the grave.

OUR STORY

We met in college, at a small, historically black university called North Carolina Agricultural and Technical State University. We were both from small towns and the first of our families to attend and graduate from a university. We met on the first day of classes in Biology 101. We instantly connected and often saw each other, as most of our classes were together. Throughout the first two years of college, we became good friends. At various points in our friendship, however, the typical physical urges arose. Sexual purity was not something either of us valued during the early years of college. Each of us at different times tried to take our friendship to a sexual level; however, our timing was never in sync.

In our junior year of college, we both invited Jesus into our hearts and began to live life differently. We both took our relationship with Christ as seriously as we knew how to, and we even started a college Bible study. Working closely together in the Bible study brought a deeper, different kind of attraction that we hadn't experienced before, and we didn't know how to navigate our deep feelings through the eyes of our new and growing faith. While our spirits were willing, our flesh became weaker over time. In one weak moment, our lives were changed forever. We were pregnant. We decided to get married and raise our baby together.

We informed our parents of our fragile plans and got engaged immediately. A month later we were married in a very small, intimate wedding with a few family members and close friends. Instead of hopeful anticipation and love-filled starry eyes, we were anxiously rolling the dice without a solid game plan and with no clue about what was ahead of us on our marriage journey. Once we were married, the frailty of our foundation began to show immediately. We could have never imagined how hard married life would be.

The first few years of our marriage were so hard neither of us thought we could make it work, despite our best intentions. We were headed for divorce on the express train. Seeing a train going off a cliff and feeling helpless to stop it or redirect it is one of the worst feelings in the world. We were blind to how our pasts and backgrounds were affecting our new marriage and young family. George and I were raised in homes with completely different cultures. We were both broken people and had a lot of baggage that we brought into our marriage. We were young, broke college students. George had one more semester in school, and on top of that, we were having a baby. The odds were definitely stacked against us. We had issues, and our issues had issues. Everything happened so fast. We had no time to really count the cost of what we had signed up for.

By the grace of God, we figured out how to make our marriage work. Once we developed our marriage game plan, the light bulb turned on for us. This light ignited a fire and hunger to learn more about how to make marriage work. We started attending marriage conferences and retreats regularly, reading every marriage book we could get our hands on. I (Tondra) even went back to school for a master's degree in counseling. We desired to help as many couples as we could to learn and grow from our mistakes. For more than twenty-five years, we have been dedicated to educating and equipping couples to have successful relationships and marriages through our ministry, Journey for Life. We believe marriage is a journey—a journey for life.

This book is for any couple out there who is lost, confused, and feeling helpless about how to make their relationship work. Marriage is hard, but there is hope. A mentor once told us, "You have a 100 percent chance of making your marriage work." To us, this means winning in our marriage is possible and doable despite challenges and tough seasons. Knowing that we can win and have a fulfilling marriage gives us the hope and determination to fight for what we desire every day. A successful marriage is not easy and requires working hard and giving 100 percent as individuals and as a couple. For two people ready and willing to put in the hard work and effort, having a game plan could change everything.

Marriage is hard, but there is hope.

THE PROBLEM

Our story fits into the larger narrative of a lot of marriages today in the United States. Many couples encounter significant challenges in sustaining their marriages despite their best intentions, desires, and love for each other. We can look at just a few marriage statistics and see how marriages end all too soon:

- The United States has the seventh-highest divorce rate in the world,[2] with 40 to 50 percent of first marriages ending with divorce.[3]
- On average, a marriage lasts eight years before a couple separates or divorces.[4]
- Sixty-seven percent of second marriages end in divorce.[5]

- Seventy-three percent of third marriages end in divorce.[6]
- In 20 percent of marriages, one person has been married before; another 20 percent of marriages are between people who have both been married before.[7]
- *Forbes* lists the three top causes for divorce as follows: 58 percent of couples attribute "arguing and excess conflict" as the cause of their divorce; 45 percent say "they married too young"; 38 percent cite financial issues as the reason for their divorce.[8]
- Some estimate that the divorce rate for professional athletes is between 60 and 80 percent.[9]
- In the area where we currently live, Orange County, California (one of the wealthiest areas in the United States), the divorce rate is 72 percent, which is higher than the national rate.[10]

We desire to see strong marriages and families become the cornerstone of our society by helping couples reimagine what a lifelong and fulfilling marriage looks like. We feel we can do this by helping couples develop game plans to make their marriages and families work and thrive. Our heart in writing this book is to equip, educate, and inspire couples on their journey to have successful relationships and marriages.

We have seen this happen many times over the last twenty-five years as we've helped countless couples prepare for marriage through premarital courses that we've taught all across the country. While most couples are excited for a possible lifelong marriage, many enter those classes without a plan or understanding of how to make marriage work.

One couple who had taken our premarital class decided to do so after living together for more than ten years. Up to that point, the boyfriend could not commit to marriage because he did not have a healthy picture or model for marriage and did not believe he could be a good husband. Through the course, he learned how to develop a marriage game plan and gained an understanding of what it takes to be married. He walked away with tools that empowered him to be a husband and marry the woman of his dreams.

That couple has been married and going strong for more than twelve years. Each time we see them, they express a deep appreciation for the help they received to begin their marriage journey the right way. This "right way" was with a marriage game plan that gave them a playbook on how to approach marriage and make it work. We believe all couples can make marriage work with a solid game plan.

WHAT IS A GAME PLAN?

A game plan in general is a well-thought-out and calculated plan for navigating challenges or achieving success in a specific area. Game plans are designed by companies, sports teams, entrepreneurs, governments, and anyone else who wants to maximize their potential and bottom line. People have personal game plans to succeed in their careers, finances, personal development, retirement, health, and wellness, just to name a few areas. We believe a marriage game plan is just as important as any other game plan that you might have in life.

A marriage game plan puts you on the same page, going in the same direction. Can you imagine a football team where each player had his own game plan, running different plays and moving in different directions? How would the team win the game? In much the same way, how can a couple win in marriage if they are not executing a unified plan and moving in the same direction toward a common goal?

A marriage game plan puts you on the same page, going in the same direction.

WHAT IS A MARRIAGE GAME PLAN?

A marriage game plan is a written or agreed-upon strategy between a husband and a wife for creating a successful marriage. Couples cannot simply have a successful marriage haphazardly; they must work together to create what they envision as the end goal. This game plan for marriage is a strategic blueprint that not only helps maximize a couple's chances of marital success but also clearly defines the who, what, when, where, and why of achieving their marriage goals together. The marriage game plan consists of strategies and actionable steps to help the couple win together. Personalizing a marriage game plan requires discipline, foresight, adaptability, accountability, and a clear vision of a successful endgame.

We think a marriage game plan should consist of a few key steps or ingredients that will help any couple reach their desired outcome:

1. **Define your win.** The desire to win together in marriage is the foundation and beginning of clarity and agreement. Defining the win shows you what success looks like as an endgame picture. The success of a marriage is built on a couple's shared purpose, vision, mission, and value system.
2. **Set your goals.** Goal setting involves taking active steps to achieve your desired outcome of winning in your marriage. Clearly defining how you envision a successful marriage will then lead you to set clear goals and objectives as a couple to achieve your endgame picture. Couples win when there are indicators and benchmarks to measure their progress and success.
3. **Know your team.** Knowing your team helps you assess teammates' differences, strengths, gifts, and growth areas. Teams that capitalize on their strengths and unique talents, while also navigating and resolving differences that could potentially create division, have the potential to achieve significant victories together.
4. **Know the opponents to your team's success.** Couples must be able to identify key opponents (obstacles, enemies, patterns, mindsets) that stand in the way of their desired outcome in marriage. Where there is a strong desire to win in marriage, there will also be fierce opponents that will attempt to upend the plan.
5. **Design your plan of action.** Designing a tactical game plan or plan of action will help a couple achieve their goals. The plan of action should be consistently practiced, reviewed, and updated to see the couple win.

When couples clearly define the wins and goals in their overall marriage and relationship, they have something to work toward together as a team and family. We want to encourage all couples to work toward having a fantastic, satisfying marriage. Far too many couples have failed to move beyond a marriage that falls short of their expectations.

In our work as NFL chaplains over the last fifteen years, we've learned that professional athletes go beyond the average to become great or play at the highest levels of success. They have sacrificed and worked hard toward their goal of making it to the professional level, which separates them from the rest. The same should be true in marriage. Healthy couples desire to create a successful marriage at the highest level and quality possible. Their goal to have a successful marriage drives everything they say and do.

There is a vast array of topics and categories that can be included in your marriage game plan. It would be impossible to cover every potential topic and category to put into a game plan in this resource alone. Within *The Marriage Game Plan*, we will go over several key categories and topics we've found both helpful and challenging throughout our thirty-year marriage.

1. **Communication strategy:** Developing clear and open channels of communication helps foster honest discussions about feelings, expectations, and concerns in the relationship.
2. **Conflict-resolution techniques:** Improving conflict-resolution skills by promoting open communication, listening to understand, and embracing compromise sets the tone for relational harmony.
3. **Friendship and intimacy:** Making time to build and nurture friendship and intimacy is key to laying a solid foundation.
4. **Fun and recreation:** Carving out time for mutual hobbies and adventures injects vitality, excitement, and pleasure into the relationship, keeping it vibrant and engaging.
5. **Intimacy and affection:** Fostering an atmosphere of physical and emotional intimacy helps cultivate a lasting bond and deeper connection.
6. **Safety and trust:** Establishing an environment of safety and trust within the relationship enhances vulnerability and transparency.

7. **Gratitude and appreciation:** Extending gratitude and showing appreciation helps create an environment of honor and mutual respect.
8. **Forgiveness:** Learning to seek and grant forgiveness lays the foundation for resolving conflict, showing compassion, and fighting for unity.
9. **Financial planning:** Setting smart financial goals and plans helps create a future of security and stability.
10. **Couples counseling or professional help:** Seeking professional guidance, including individual and couples therapy, sets couples up to achieve marital success.
11. **Spiritual agreement:** Understanding and embracing God's design and purpose for marriage provides couples with a firm foundation upon which they can build their marriage and game plan.

Other areas of consideration outside the scope of this book may include:

Roles and responsibilities	Individual growth and support
Family planning	Continuous evaluation and adjustment
Health and wellness	Social connections
Continual learning and growth	Legacy building

Remember, every marriage is unique, so it's essential to have a customized game plan according to your specific needs, dynamics, and goals. Additionally, flexibility and willingness to adapt are crucial for navigating the ups and downs of married life effectively. By incorporating these components into a marriage game plan, couples can build a strong foundation for a fulfilling and enduring partnership that withstands the test of time.

Within each chapter of *The Marriage Game Plan*, we share our stories, joys, struggles, and ups and downs from throughout our marriage journey. We are not experts because we've gotten it all right throughout our marriage. Just the opposite is true. We've learned a lot of things the hard way, through trial and error, and by simply making mistakes. We hope you can learn from our transparency and willingness to be vulnerable. In addition to sharing our stories and our love for helping couples have successful marriages, we've framed many of our marriage tools and strategies around sports themes from our work as chaplains with professional athletes and coaches. There are countless sports-related metaphors and analogies to help you win in your marriage.

Our goal is not for you to simply read our book on marriage and stop there. We hope that by the time you finish reading each chapter, you will be ready to develop and work on a marriage game plan with your spouse that will help you win in your marriage. In the "Putting It into Practice" section at the end of each chapter, we welcome you to work on your marriage game plan by completing a set of questions and activities with your spouse. These questions and activities will require time and effort to complete; however, it is a worthy investment into your marriage. Answering the questions and participating in the activities with your spouse will get you on the same page. We've even given you a place to list personal and collective action items that you want to implement from the reading, questions, and activities.

As an added bonus, each chapter includes an opportunity for you to dive deeper into developing your marriage game plan. You'll have access to a short "Time-Out" video where we explore key segments of the chapter's content, offering further insights and practical tips. The videos are accessible through a URL and QR code at the end of each chapter.

The fun does not stop there. The final chapter is your opportunity to personalize and develop your marriage game plan together after you've read each chapter, answered the questions, watched the "Time-Out" bonus videos, and completed the Couple's Activities. Chapter 10 integrates key aspects from your work throughout the book, such as marriage coaching tips, which recap important takeaways and action items to implement in your marriage. The final chapter will also guide you to insert and refer to essential elements from the questions and activities throughout the book to formulate your specific marriage game plan. These activity items, action steps, and tips will combine to form your unique game plan that you can continue to build on and adjust as you grow and evolve as individuals and as a couple for many years to come. Consider your marriage game plan as a work in progress throughout your relationship.

We recommend waiting to complete chapter 10 after you have done all the reading, questions, and activities from chapters 1 through 9. This will allow chapter 10 to serve as a recap and reflection of all the things you've learned and worked on throughout the book. The summary in the final chapter is critical to developing your marriage game plan.

Done right, a well-laid-out marriage game plan helps put couples on the same page and keeps them going in the same direction. It also gives them a plan for success. A mentor once reminded us, "If you fail to plan, then your plan is to fail." This chapter will become your strategic plan of action and catalyst to give your marriage game plan life and launch you and your spouse on a clear path to growing and winning together. Are you ready? Let's go!

Putting It into Practice

QUESTIONS

1. What impacted you most from this chapter, and why?

2. What do you hope to gain from reading this book?

3. Which game plan topics and categories mentioned in this chapter are strengths in your marriage? Which ones are areas for growth?

Reflect on the journey of your love story as a couple.

- What brought you together?

- Why did you choose to commit to each other?

- What challenges were present?

- What makes your love story special and worth fighting for?

COUPLE'S ACTIVITY
CRAFTING A MARRIAGE VISION STATEMENT

A marriage vision statement captures what you want your marriage to become and what legacy you aim to leave for future generations. If couples are going to be successful in their marriage, they must know their why, purpose, and end goal.

Take a moment to compile a list outlining the specific ways you envision or dream of your marriage unfolding over the next fifty to sixty years. Consider the big picture, and visualize the ultimate outcome you desire for your marriage. Each spouse should do this separately. Then share and discuss your answers with each other.

To help you get started brainstorming possible ways you want to win in your marriage, we've listed a few key categories to consider:

- Fidelity and commitment
- Trust and communication
- Respect and support
- Quality time and shared experiences
- Love and affection
- Partnership and teamwork
- Intimacy and connection

Here are examples of two marriage vision statements:

Our marriage vision is to honor God and each other by fulfilling the covenants we made to each other on our wedding day. We desire to cultivate a deep friendship and love, remaining faithful to each other in all that we say and do. We aspire to have a home filled with joy, peace, and unwavering support, where we can be our best as individuals and as a couple.

As a married couple, we will strive to make it through all things and win together no matter what we face. We seek transparent communication based on love, mutual respect, and unity. We desire to leave a godly legacy of marriage for our children and future generations to come.

WRITE YOUR MARRIAGE VISION STATEMENT

CRAFTING A MARRIAGE MISSION STATEMENT

A marriage mission statement is a succinct declaration outlining how you as a couple will live your lives together to accomplish your marriage vision. A strong marriage mission statement encompasses concrete actions and decisions that both of you commit to. These actions and decisions should be rooted in your shared values and principles. Having a clear mission statement will keep you moving in the same direction as a couple.

Take a moment to compile a list of the values that you aspire to uphold on your marriage journey. These values will be your guide and a critical part of your marriage playbook throughout your journey together. Examples of values you may want to include are love, forgiveness, commitment, dedication, trust, faithfulness, sacrifice, compassion, affection, devotion, appreciation, loyalty, friendship, desire, harmony, joy, intimacy, and laughter.

List three meaningful values to be included in your marriage mission statement below. Feel free to use any of the values listed above.

You can also craft your mission statement by deciding together how to answer a few important questions:

- How do we want to treat each other throughout our marriage?
- How do we build a relationship of fidelity and faithfulness?
- How do we intend to tackle obstacles and resolve conflicts as a team?
- How will we commit to building trust, healthy communication, and mutual respect in our relationship?
- How do we intend to sustain intimacy, connection, and romance within our marriage?

YOUR MARRIAGE MISSION STATEMENT

Here are examples of two marriage mission statements:

> We desire to win in our marriage by expressing our love in action, seeking to understand and grant forgiveness, and committing to lifelong covenant communication.

> We desire to win in our marriage by supporting each other, growing in our friendship, and building a strong foundation of trust, respect, and communication.

WRITE YOUR MARRIAGE MISSION STATEMENT

We desire to win in our marriage by

PRAYER POINTS TO CONSIDER

ACTION ITEMS

(What steps, actions, or decisions do you need to make or take?)

TIME-OUT

For further insights and practical tips from this chapter, take a time-out and view our short bonus video, "Time-Out: The Importance of a Game Plan," using this link or QR code:

https://davidccook.org/access

Access code: GamePlan

Chapter 2

THE PLAYBOOK ON MARRIAGE

When the mind is controlled and spirit aligned with purpose, the body is capable of so much more than we realize.

Rich Roll

The real challenge of having a successful marriage in our contemporary society is essentially a genuine misunderstanding of why marriage was designed originally. To get the most out of any valuable product we buy from the store, we must understand why its designer created it. To get this information, we must first look at the owner's manual, as it will clearly define what the product is and why it was created.

Many owner's manuals also include a section on what a product was *not* created for or warnings about misusing the product. For example, you would not go into an electronics store and purchase the latest and fastest laptop to help you organize your life without first knowing how it will help you accomplish your goal. You would not take the expensive laptop home and use it as a hammer, a trivet for a hot pot, or a lid when microwaving food. Those are simply not purposes for which the computer was created and designed.

To have a thriving and successful marriage that is able to stand the test of time, we must understand why its Creator designed it in the first place. To find that out, we must go to the Designer of marriage, God, and go back to the owner's manual on marriage, the Holy Bible, for help. But the Bible is much more than an owner's manual where you can find out what God had in mind when He created marriage.

Another way we can view the Bible is as a playbook that has been designed by God (we'll talk more about this in the next chapter). Within the Bible's sacred pages lie answers, strategies, and best practices to help us win in our marriages if we will simply follow the plays within. The Bible is the best playbook on marriage that we can use. It is impossible to construct our marriage game plans without understanding God's game plan and heart for marriage. So, what was God's heart and mind as He created marriage? We are glad you asked!

GOD'S GAME PLAN OR PURPOSE FOR MARRIAGE

When we think of God's original idea of marriage, we are mainly asking, "What ultimate picture did God have in mind as the end goal?" Knowing what God had in mind when He created marriage will give us a better chance at replicating that image as couples. Not having that image in mind will lead us to completely distort God's original image and plan. As fallen humans, we have way too often made up our own snapshots of what things are supposed to be and have gotten way off course.

One could compare trying to replicate or reproduce God's ultimate picture of marriage to the mystery of attempting to put a sixty-thousand-piece jigsaw puzzle together without the picture on the box top. No one likes to put jigsaw puzzles together more than Tondra and I do. We enjoy seeing the puzzle pieces fit together with similar shapes and patterns to make the picture come alive, just like the image on the puzzle's box top.

But can you imagine putting together an intricate sixty-thousand-piece jigsaw puzzle without having the complete picture from the box top? Even the most avid puzzle enthusiasts would feel frustrated and confused about how all the puzzle pieces fit together as they were designed to if they didn't have the box-top image. So imagine how overwhelmed most married couples feel attempting to put the pieces of a successful relationship together without the end picture. Fortunately, we don't have to guess how to put the puzzle called marriage together properly. We have the end-goal picture of marriage given to us in the Bible.

While we cannot include an exhaustive list of all the purposes God created marriage for, in this chapter we will go over four main purposes God had in mind. From these four we can get a better understanding of how to make marriage work according to its original design. In this chapter we will go over God's heart to:

- establish a lifelong promise of love and commitment,
- build a team of oneness and solidarity,
- provide a companion and helper, and
- reflect God's image to the world.

ESTABLISH A LIFELONG PROMISE OF LOVE AND COMMITMENT

One of God's intended purposes for marriage was to establish a lifelong promise of love and commitment between a husband and a wife. Without a lifelong promise of love and commitment in marriage, there would be nothing separating it from any other serious adult relationship. During most wedding ceremonies there is a time when the bride and groom exchange wedding vows or make promises in front of God and their family and friends. The words of the vows might differ from couple to couple, but the heart of the vows is a promise to honor, love, and cherish each other; to work together; to remain faithful to each other; and to commit to a lifelong marriage. Traditional wedding vows might include promises like these:

"I take you to be my wedded wife/husband"
"to have and to hold"
"from this day forward"
"for better or for worse"
"for richer or for poorer"
"in sickness and in health"
"to love and to cherish"
"till death do us part"

These sacred vows essentially establish a covenant between a husband and a wife, much like the covenant or promise between Christ and His church. Covenants and promises are not meant to be easily broken as times become hard or circumstances change. Covenants are meant to have permanence and security that will not fade or lose their brilliancy over time. When it comes to the ultimate example of a lifelong promise of love, sacrifice, and commitment to the end, there is no better image than that of Christ's pursuit of His church.

> As the Scriptures say, "A man leaves his father and mother and is joined to his wife, and the two are united into one." This is a great mystery, but it is an illustration of the way Christ and the church are one. (Eph. 5:31–32 NLT)

This great mystery that Paul is referring to is the comparison of the relationship between a husband and a wife to that of Christ and His church. Ephesians 5 points to a perfect display of Christ's unyielding sacrificial love, even to the point of death. All this for the sake of His bride, the church. Christ endured all this painstaking suffering and sacrifice so that He could prepare His bride to spend eternity together with Him. In the same way, husbands and wives are also required to establish a lifelong promise of love and commitment through the marriage covenant:

> For husbands, this means love your wives, just as Christ loved the church. He gave up his life for her.... Husbands ought to love their wives as they love their own bodies. For a man who loves his wife actually shows love for himself. No one hates his own body but feeds and cares for it, just as Christ cares for the church....
>
> So again I say, each man must love his wife as he loves himself, and the wife must respect her husband. (vv. 25, 28–29, 33 NLT)

This is a critical puzzle piece of the complete image that God had in mind when He created marriage between a husband and a wife. We cannot have a successful marriage without an undying promise of love and commitment like Christ gives His church. Our marriages must have unyielding and unconditional sacrificial love that can stand the test of time. This type of love and commitment are expressed in the vows and promises we make on our wedding day. These vows and promises are essentially covenants that we establish and set out to honor "till death do us part."

Millions of couples every year plan and have weddings. These weddings usually cost a lot of time, energy, and money. Family and friends are invited to celebrate a couple's special day of memorializing their love and commitment to each other. Vows and promises are shared in the presence of God and everyone in attendance. The bride and groom pronounce their love and plans to live together and spend the rest of their lives as one. These vows are spoken in terms of permanence, longevity, and sincerity. We've never heard vows that forecast a fickle or unstable future or a lack of commitment and devotion. Not once has anyone promised to end their covenant at the first sign of trouble or when times get hard.

During traditional wedding ceremonies, what follows the exchange of vows is the exchange of wedding rings by both spouses. While many people focus on the beauty, size, or cost of the wedding rings, the meaning of the wedding ring is much deeper. The giving of rings during the wedding ceremony is a permanent outward sign, symbol, and reminder of the marriage covenant established on the wedding day. The ring is a token of love and faithfulness. It is a circle that has no beginning or end and is symbolic of God's eternal love for us. The rings are meant to be a constant reminder to each spouse of the type of love and commitment expressed on the wedding day.

When we first started out in marriage, we did not totally understand what these vows or promises meant or the weight they carried. In all the weddings that we'd attended in support of others, these vows had always been a part of the ceremony, so we chose to say the same words as others. While we tried as best as we could to mean them on our wedding day, these words would come back to challenge us throughout the course of our marriage, mainly because living them is easier said than done. Marriage is not easy. We often say marriage is a rough team sport. And yet we promised each other and made a covenant that we would love and commit to each other through all circumstances and seasons.

We often ask couples who are having marital problems to pull out their wedding ceremony video or pictures from that day and relive the moment they made those sacred vows and promises. It's not enough to say "I do." That's the easy part. The challenging part is to say "I still do" through all the ups and downs and good and not-so-good days. Remembering the promises and covenants that we made on our wedding days can be a great way to refocus on what God originally had in mind when He created marriage.

BUILD A TEAM OF ONENESS AND SOLIDARITY

Throughout the Bible, God illustrates that one of His main reasons for creating the institution of marriage was to bring two people together in oneness and solidarity. By oneness and solidarity, we mean God brings two separate, individual lives together to create one new unit that is focused on unity; marriage provides a togetherness and teamwork that staying single cannot afford. It unites two unique people with different upbringings, backgrounds, likes, dislikes, and everything in between. Oneness is an essential ingredient to a happy and healthy marriage.

> "For this reason a man shall leave his father and mother and be joined to his wife, and the two shall become one flesh"; so then they are no longer two, but one flesh. Therefore what God has joined together, let not man separate. (Mark 10:7–9 NKJV)

This well-known passage highlights God's intention to bring a man and a woman so closely together as one that nothing can separate the two. Not even the familial bond between a parent and a child, or any other human relationship, can come in between their oneness. The man is required to leave his mother and father and be joined to his new wife. The phrase *joined together* literally means "to fasten to one yoke,… to join together, unite."[1] The intention is a bond not to be broken, divided, or separated. Some people think marriage is just a piece of paper or a contract, but that is not God's intention. Marriage is a sacred bond between two people. One of the best parts about marriage is being spiritually glued or connected to your lifelong companion and helper with the help of almighty God.

The bond between a husband and a wife is so close that despite the fact they are two different people, through their new union, they are as "one flesh" or team (Mark 10:8 NKJV). "One flesh" is symbolic of the oneness that God originally intended when He created the first marriage between Adam and Eve. You cannot become one and create a marriage of oneness haphazardly or accidentally. You build oneness and solidarity only with intentionality and daily choices.

When we were first married, we had to establish this intentionality, as we did not recognize this important step initially. It took some time for us to realize that our disagreements were mostly due to our selfish, independent, and individual ways of looking at things. We had to embrace our newly formed team and work together as one unit instead of two separate people. This meant purposefully allowing each other to shape and influence each other through our different perspectives and ways of tackling problems.

I (George) needed a lot of help in this area. Even though it was clearly apparent I did not have all the answers and could not solve every problem in our new marriage, I tried to act as if I had it all figured out. Isn't that what a husband is supposed to do? Have all the right answers and know everything? My fear of not measuring up and my need to always be right did not create opportunities for oneness and teamwork. Tondra often felt that she had been shut down and her opinion overlooked.

One time we were pulling into our driveway, and I was driving Tondra's car. We had a two-car garage, but instead of parking her car in the garage beside my car, I chose to park her car in the driveway. Tondra asked me if it was wise to leave her car in the driveway because I might end up having to go somewhere in my car. I assured her that I had it all under control. Later that evening—you guessed it!—I forgot her car was behind my car in the driveway and I sideswiped it. I had not been intentional about listening to her ideas then, and it cost me big time. I wish that was the only time.

Another time, we were driving home from an event, and I got lost but could not bring myself to tell her I did not know how to get us home. After thirty minutes of wrong turns and dead ends, Tondra asked if I would just pull over at a gas station and ask for directions. She had no clue she was asking me to give up my man card by asking for help with directions. I was simply too prideful to ask for assistance. I did not want to admit that I did not have the answer or allow my wife to help me solve this problem. In the end, a trip that should have taken only forty minutes actually took us two hours! Thank God, we men now have Google Maps and other ways of not having to admit we need help with directions.

These are just small examples of a bigger problem that I brought into our marriage. I have since learned that a husband does not have to have all the answers. In fact, we need help in life from our God-given helper. I will share more on this in the next section. I have learned to ask for help and embrace Tondra's viewpoints and opinions. I must admit, life has not been the same for me since I learned to be intentional and embrace oneness and our marriage team daily.

We know from personal experience that becoming one in marriage is not an easy task. It takes time, and often many newlywed couples desire this oneness to happen instantly on their wedding night or during their first year of marriage. But sometimes it takes more time than we think. The main goal is to develop a desire and heart to become one with your spouse. This oneness happens over time as each spouse daily makes intentional decisions to become one.

PROVIDE A COMPANION AND HELPER

If there is one thing that marriage has taught us, it is that we were not meant to walk through life alone. We are not saying that everyone is meant to be married or that anyone should get married without doing the hard work of preparing for a potential spouse. When the time is right, we believe God will bring the right person into your life, just as He did for Adam in the garden of Eden. Genesis 2 has a few verses that clearly show God's intention to give us a companion and helper:

> The LORD God said, "It is not good for the man to be alone. I will make a helper suitable for him." …
>
> But for Adam no suitable helper was found. So the LORD God caused the man to fall into a deep sleep; and while he was sleeping, he took one of the man's ribs and then closed up the place with flesh. Then the LORD God made a woman from the rib he had taken out of the man, and he brought her to the man. (vv. 18, 20–22)

What a beautiful image of God's heart for humanity, that He would design, create, and bring a spouse who was a helper and partner for Adam to become his best self.

In these verses, we clearly see that Adam was doing fine. He had a job and his own place to live, but God saw something was missing in his life. It was then that God decided that being alone was not best for Adam, so He made a helper and companion who was suitable for Adam.

God made Eve to be Adam's spouse, life partner, and teammate. What a beautiful image of God's heart for humanity, that He would design, create, and bring a spouse who was a helper and partner for Adam to become his best self.

Eve was not just any woman that God brought to Adam. God's desire for Adam was to have a spouse or partner who was "suitable" for him, as the Genesis passage pointed out. Why? Because "for Adam no suitable helper was found" (v. 20). The word *suitable* here describes a proper fit or complement or opposite.[2] It refers to someone or something that would fill the gaps that Adam had. In essence, Eve was God's solution for what Adam needed in life. Eve was to help Adam accomplish all the things that he could not do solely by himself. She was his complement.

Eve was not brought to Adam to be a servant or play a subordinate role, which is what we often think of when we hear the English word *helper*. Far too many men and women have gotten this wrong. The Hebrew word translated "helper" here is the same word used to describe how God helps us as humans in our time of need. Take for instance Psalm 115:9–11, where God is not a subordinate or a servant but a great help in a desperate time when the psalmist needed divine assistance and support:

> O Israel, trust the LORD!
>   He is your helper and your shield.
> O priests, descendants of Aaron, trust the LORD!
>   He is your helper and your shield.
> All you who fear the LORD, trust the LORD!
>   He is your helper and your shield. (NLT)

No matter who you are or what stage you find yourself in on your marriage journey, if you are a spouse, you have a helper and partner in life and marriage. Take a moment to let that sink in. Your spouse is your God-given helper, teammate, complement, and partner. You don't have to walk alone, nor should you ever feel like you are the Lone Ranger riding solo. In order for us to get the most out of having a helper and teammate, we must accept and embrace the strengths and gifts they have to offer us. Accepting and embracing what they bring to the table helps create oneness.

But let's take that a step further. You don't just have a helper; you are also a helper to your spouse. Just as we need help and partnership, we must also be a helper and partner to our spouses. Many times in marriage we totally miss this point. Some men think that women were created to be a one-sided helper for the man. Some women feel like a man's role is to be the sole helper, provider, and everything for the family. Both views are shortsighted and do not fully express God's heart for bringing two people together.

In God's game plan for marriage, He knew we as humans, both male and female, needed a teammate to walk with us in life and help us. He also knew we could be helpers for our spouses. That is why you will constantly hear us saying throughout this book, "We are on the same team." Being successfully married requires a team mentality, not an individualistic mindset. This is a piece of the marriage puzzle that many couples are missing. We are better together because we can help each other when times get tough or when we need someone to pick us up. God knows life is challenging and two people walking together in love and unity are better than one person facing life alone.

As spouses, we are in our marriages to help each other succeed, to fight our opponents together, and to comfort and encourage each other. Sometimes it's easy to dismiss our spouses when we think we can do life on our own. Or when we question what they bring to the table and if they can help us at all. The reality is none of us are perfect and none of us can live life solely on our own without help, guidance, and comfort.

REFLECT GOD'S IMAGE TO THE WORLD

When God created men and women, He did not make us in a way that was detached and unfamiliar with His divine nature and purpose. In fact, God created men and women to look like and act like Him in His divine nature. Genesis says: "So God created man in his own image, in the image of God he created him; male and female he created them" (1:27 ESV).

Before you think this idea of humans being made in God's image and likeness is a little far-fetched, just take a moment and remember your youth. As kids we are often told we resemble and act like our parents. I was often called "Little Henry Gregory" because I had features just like my father. It wasn't just that I looked almost like his twin, but I took on his mannerisms and the way that he carried himself as well. Even though people's comments got on my nerves when I was growing up as a boy, I did look and sound like my dad in many ways. As I've gotten older, I've even done many things just like my father. I chose ministry as a career, married one woman and remained faithful to her, and raised my family to honor God.

> We like to say that marriage is God's best selfie.

Just as we look and often act like our earthly parents, we resemble and display the characteristics, likeness, and attributes of our heavenly Father. As individuals, we are created in His image, but every married couple should desperately desire to reflect God's image and characteristics to our spouse, family, and those around us in a greater manner. Marriage was created for more than our happiness as a couple. In marriage, a husband and wife help reflect God's image and nature to the community and world around us. We think this is a major piece of the puzzle called marriage that is missing in our contemporary culture.

Image is very important today. We live in a selfie generation where we take lots of pictures of ourselves until we get the image that reflects our best self. We might take ten pictures, but we post only the one picture that displays us in the best way. In the same way, God's intention for marriage and family is to reflect His best picture to the world. His image is seen through the family. We like to say that marriage is God's best selfie.

As couples who have committed to a lifelong marriage, we can show the world what Christlike love, forgiveness, sacrifice, and commitment mean through our marriage covenant. Ephesians 5 says these attributes were modeled by Christ Himself as the bridegroom to His bride, the church. We briefly discussed this earlier in the section on marriage as a lifelong promise of love and commitment. As we said before, marriage, although rewarding, is not always easy and can bring out the good and bad tendencies in all of us.

In fact, marriage is one of the best places to practice being more like Christ as there are countless moments of testing. Ask any husband or wife and they will tell you the fruits of our human nature are not easy to subdue and often want to surface. They often come out in the form of our sinful nature, or what Galatians 5:19 calls "the acts of the flesh." The works of the flesh are often characterized as strife, jealousy, fits of anger, selfish ambition, rivalries, dissensions, divisions, and envy. Instead of allowing the works of the flesh to dominate our marriages, we should desire to display "the fruit of the Spirit" in our relationship (Gal. 5:22). The fruit of the Spirit is "love, joy, peace, patience, kindness, goodness, faithfulness, gentleness, and self-control" (vv. 22–23 NLT).

The saying "You know a tree by the fruit it bears" is true with the fruit of the Spirit. As couples, we have an indication of how well we are doing displaying the fruit of the Spirit or the works of the flesh by how we treat each other daily in our communication and response to each other. If we are constantly arguing, having fits of rage, or living with dissension and divisions, then deep down inside we know we are not reflecting God's true image to our family or the people around us. To reflect His image to a world that is hurting and looking for hope, we have to display marriages full of the fruit of the Spirit as mentioned in the previous paragraph. This takes a lot of practice.

The big question is this: Does your marriage pass the litmus test of properly reflecting God's image to those around us as He intended? We cannot bear or display God's true character without being in a close relationship with Him daily through praying, worshipping, and reading His Word. As we worship, pray, and read God's Word, we will get to know Him more by learning His character and nature. In turn, we will act like Him more and more. The truth is, the more we hang around someone who influences us, the more people around us can tell.

One day, I (George) was preparing to put my son Jay in bed for the evening before Tondra came home. I asked him to go upstairs and get ready for bed. Before I could get upstairs to say prayers with him and tuck him in, Tondra came in the door. As always, when she arrived, I gave her a big hug and a few passionate kisses before I headed upstairs. Jay still had no clue that she was home until I hugged and kissed him for bed. All of a sudden, Jay said in a loud voice, "Ew! You smell just like Mom!" Tondra's perfume smell gave him an indication that I had been spending time with her as her perfume had rubbed off on me. The same is true when we spend time with God in worship, prayer, and His Word. People around us can tell we've been spending time with God because His nature, character, and even aroma rub off on us.

> *God has given us His heart, design, and purpose for marriage.*

In marriage, we can indeed display and reflect God's image to others around us by how we treat each other. How we relate to, love, forgive, show compassion to, value, and esteem each other is very important. As couples, we are called to walk together and show the world the love that Christ showed us: "Be kind and compassionate to one another, forgiving each other, just as in Christ God forgave you" (Eph. 4:32).

As couples who desire to have successful marriages and relationships, one of the worst things we can do is to make up our own game plan when it comes to marriage. To make marriage work without proper planning is a puzzling and daunting task to say the least. Thankfully, we don't have to make up a blueprint or guess at it. God has given us His heart, design, and purpose for marriage. Understanding and embracing God's design and purpose for marriage provides couples with a firm foundation on which they can build their marriage and game plan. If we follow His heart and design, we are well on our way to learning how to win the home game.

Putting It into Practice

QUESTIONS

1. What impacted you most from this chapter, and why?

2. What is the significance of the term *helper* in our culture's perception of marriage, and how is being a helper valued? Please list three specific areas in your life where you currently need help or support from your spouse.

3. Share with your spouse a moment when their support filled a void in your life. Convey your heartfelt gratitude and appreciation for their assistance and the profound impact it had on you.

4. Every married couple should have a strong desire to reflect God's image to those around us in a greater manner. Does your marriage reflect God's image to those around you? Take a moment to make a list of godly characteristics you want to reflect to others. Then, share one thing you will personally commit to doing to make this happen.

5. What are the challenges that make it difficult to foster unity and oneness within a marriage?

6. In the previous chapter activity, together you came up with a list of some ways you wanted your relationship to be successful. Do these goals align with God's purposes for marriage as outlined in this chapter? If not, consider making some adjustments.

COUPLE'S ACTIVITY: RENEW YOUR WEDDING VOWS

Please take a moment to locate and read the wedding vows (covenants) that you made to each other on your wedding day. Is there anything that needs to be adjusted or rewritten after reading chapter 2? If so, please take time to rewrite them. Finally, take a few minutes and renew your vows to your spouse as a way of reaffirming your commitment to each other.

PRAYER POINTS TO CONSIDER

ACTION ITEMS
(What steps, actions, or decisions do you need to make or take?)

TIME-OUT

For further insights and practical tips from this chapter, take a time-out and view our short bonus video, "Time-Out: The Playbook on Marriage," using this link or QR code:

https://davidccook.org/access
Access code: GamePlan

Chapter 3

WINNING THE HOME GAME

The way a team plays as a whole determines its success. You may have the greatest bunch of individual stars in the world, but if they don't play together, the club won't be worth a dime.

Babe Ruth

A large part of what George and I do is teach professional athletes, coaches, and their families how to win at home, not just on the field. As couples, you can learn from athletes and sports teams how to win your home game by utilizing some of their strategies for winning on the field. Athletes win because they have the right mindset and attitude, study and know the playbook, commit to a lifestyle of discipline, and recognize the importance of practice as well as rest and recovery. Here are some things we learned from the pros.

We will never forget that in 2020 the world experienced a pandemic. We were quarantined and locked down. A lot of things we had once taken for granted were stripped away. We were out of control. We were socially isolated from our friends, extended family, and work colleagues. We had to take on new roles, such as homeschool teachers for our kids, Zoom experts for work, home chefs, baristas, personal trainers, and more.

The world as we knew it was shaken up like a snow globe. When the fake snow gets stirred up, the image in the globe gets blurry. When this happens, it's difficult to see the image as clearly as you saw it before. As couples, we get tested by shake-ups, whether it be career challenges, financial issues, health concerns, marital conflict, or parenting dilemmas. These shake-ups and stressors can cloud our view, preventing us from clearly seeing the road ahead or the plan for navigating through these challenges.

No matter what pressures or stresses couples face, how we respond to the shake-ups in our lives is vitally important. Stress has a way of revealing and exploiting the cracks in the foundation of a relationship. Stressful times can deteriorate our perspective and the quality of a relationship over time because of their negative impact on us physically, mentally, relationally, and emotionally. The challenge is not letting stress tear you apart but allowing it to pull you closer together.

The choice is yours: How will you allow difficult situations to impact you and your relationship? Will you blame and resent each other, isolate, shut down, not communicate, and turn away from each other? Or will you turn toward each other as teammates, fighting for unity and healthy communication and utilizing your strengths to build each other up to win in your relationship and home? To "win" in your relationship is to be on the same page, accomplish your goals, encourage each other, and allow each person to grow. We want to give you some tips and strategies for winning the home game together.

BETTER TOGETHER

The first thing you need to know as a couple is that you are better together. You are not alone in life's ups and downs. You and your spouse are teammates. When one loses, you both lose, and when one wins, you both win. As husbands and wives, you are no longer independent but rather interdependent.

Interdependence means recognizing your need for each other and allowing each person to shape, grow, and lean on the other throughout life's journey. Interdependence is the mark of a healthy relationship because it brings balance, and balance is health. The problem is our culture validates and glorifies independence, which makes interdependence seem like weakness or incompetence.

On the contrary, interdependence is a superpower when it comes to relationships, and independence undermines the whole purpose of marriage. Interdependence allows both partners and the relationship to thrive and shine their brightest, while independence causes competition and division, which can lead to the death and defeat of a relationship. I (Tondra) come from a history of strong black women who taught me that independence and self-sufficiency are a sign of strength and the only way to survive in this world. Needing a person or help was a weakness. I learned early to rely on myself and pull myself up by my own bootstraps.

This mindset created a barrier between George and me that would not allow us to come together as a team and grow deeper in our relationship. This mindset caused George to feel unneeded and devalued. Everyone desires significance and value in a relationship. Interdependence brings this extremely important ingredient to the marriage. You are better together.

> *As husbands and wives, you are no longer independent but rather interdependent.*

There is a caveat to this component that cannot be left unsaid: interdependence does not mean you are dependent on each other. Dependence will drive the relationship into an unhealthy, toxic pattern, which will also undermine the whole purpose of marriage. Dependence in a relationship causes partners to lean on each other to fulfill needs their partner was never designed to fulfill and does not have the power to meet—for example, trying to heal my trust issues by expecting George to always be in my eyesight and presence. Or his consistently having to prove his faithfulness when we are not together physically. This is unrealistic. Dependence in a relationship could also look like one spouse being the giver and the other spouse being the taker. Both the giver and the taker are attempting to feel loved and valued. The giver builds self-worth by being needed, and the taker receives self-worth by being fixed or rescued by their spouse. Both put extreme pressure on each other and the relationship, creating a dysfunctional relationship dynamic.

Successful teams know how to work together. When a team goes up against their opponent in a game, they are more successful when they work together, each one bringing their strengths and talents as well as doing their part to support the team toward the larger, common goal.

Ecclesiastes 4 includes a popular passage that's used in many weddings:

> Two people are better off than one, for they can help each other succeed. If one person falls, the other can reach out and help. But someone who falls alone is in real trouble.... A person standing alone can be attacked and defeated, but two can stand back-to-back and conquer. (vv. 9–10, 12 NLT)

This passage says, in marriage, you are not alone, and that's a good thing because two people together have a better chance of surviving and overcoming obstacles and challenges. Being better together doesn't apply just to the good times when things are fun and easy but even more to the hard, challenging times. The image from the passage of two people "stand[ing] back-to-back," ready to "conquer" (v. 12), reminds me of *Mr. & Mrs. Smith*, a great movie starring Angelina Jolie and Brad Pitt.

Mr. and Mrs. Smith are top-secret spy assassins who have bounties on their heads because their competitors found out they are married. Their marriage is a threat because together they are more powerful, so all the other top spies are trying to kill them. In one scene, Mr. and Mrs. Smith are backed into a corner surrounded by their enemies. They stand back-to-back, with multiple guns locked and loaded. Mr. and Mrs. Smith work together, fending off the enemy, holding each other's lives in their hands, and trusting each other. Imagine the scene something like synchronized swimming, except with automatic weapons. Excluding the blood and violence, it is a beautiful scene showcasing a couple united as a team in battle against their adversaries. Utilizing everything they have, Mr. and Mrs. Smith ensure each other's survival.[1]

The movie is an extreme depiction of the real-life, day-to-day struggles couples face. Success is found when couples realize they are better together no matter what kind of pressures and stresses they are up against in their lives. Can you imagine if Mr. and Mrs. Smith had been focused on each other rather than the enemy and had been hypercritical of each other? "Are you sure you got this? That's not how you hold that! You're always grabbing the wrong gun." The enemy would have easily taken them out. The key to a successful marriage is being able to stand back-to-back and conquer. It's you and your spouse against the problem, standing back-to-back against divorce, unforgiveness, bitterness—against all the enemies who seek to divide and conquer you as a couple.

In the movie *Gladiator*, Maximus (the main character) and other condemned criminals are forced to fight as gladiators in the arena as entertainment for the Roman Empire. Of course, the condemned prisoners are expected to be defeated, but there is a scene where Maximus rallies all the prisoners to work as a team. He says, "We've got a better chance of survival if we work together.... If we stay together, we survive!"[2]

The same goes for marriage. If the Enemy can get you to turn on each other, blame each other, or be self-focused or selfish, then you can be defeated. All your hopes and dreams as a couple and family, your children's peace, and God's purpose and plans will be thwarted. It takes humility to accept and admit you need each other.

MENTAL TOUGHNESS

It's easy to be together, but it's a lot harder to be *better* together. When there was too much togetherness during the pandemic, it made things more challenging. Being better together requires mental toughness. Mental toughness is about training and preparing yourself to be mentally ready for whatever challenge comes your way. When couples are mentally ready, they are able to push past failure, hurt, and fears. This allows couples to remain hopeful, positive, and ready to succeed.

Life is like a marathon, not a sprint. Knowing there's a long race filled with twists and turns before us helps us prepare and pace ourselves for the journey. We don't have control over what life brings our way, but we do have control over how we respond. We call this perspective. The ultimate perspective is that no matter what life throws at us, we will get through it if we stay together. Mental toughness is the confidence that no matter what comes your way as a couple, you have the ability, knowledge, wisdom, creativity, strength, and innovation to adjust and find a way to win or overcome.

When George and I first left the South and moved to New York City (NYC), it felt like a cross-cultural shift because the two places were extremely different. Growing up and living in North Carolina did not prepare us for navigating life in NYC. One day I was venting my frustrations to a new friend who had successfully navigated the same transition many years before. This friend gave us profound wisdom about how to feel settled in NYC. She told us, "The secret is to be ready for anything. Once you adjust to having to adjust constantly, then you have adjusted to NYC."

Feeling settled in NYC is when you are comfortable with constant change and flexibility, allowing these conditions to bring out the best in you. Your confidence must lie in your ability to figure things out and solve whatever problems each day brings. Couples also face seasons where they must live outside their comfort zones as life is constantly changing, whether it be because of health problems, career changes, finances, the need to relocate, parenting issues, or conflict. However, when couples have that mental toughness, no matter what life brings their way, they are ready to do whatever it takes to overcome the challenge. Mental toughness helps couples remain positive, not dwelling on mistakes but finding new ways to forgive, honor, accept, and give grace to each other during seasons of uncertainty and challenge.

DISCIPLINE AND PRACTICE MAKE A MARRIAGE STRONGER

Athletes understand the importance of discipline and practice in order to win. To keep their bodies and minds strong and healthy for optimal performance, athletes are disciplined about forming the right habits. They are disciplined about getting the right nutrition, studying their playbook, and ensuring they rest and recover. Cutting corners is a no-no because they understand the benefit of forgoing temporary satisfaction for long-term gains. Athletes are also disciplined about practicing and putting the work in to get better. They know that practice is essential to remain at the top of their game, that they cannot win if they don't practice. Athletes practice the way they want to play in the game because practice is what prepares them for the game.

Just like athletes, couples can maintain their mental toughness during challenging seasons of life through discipline and practice. The time to build mental toughness is not when you are already in a stressful season. Discipline and practice will help couples be ready and prepared when a major event comes, such as a career change, relocation, parenting or health issues, or financial challenges. When couples are disciplined and practice healthy habits such as clear communication, effective conflict resolution, strategic planning, and teamwork, they are better prepared to navigate every season of life at optimal levels. Your success as a couple is found in your daily routines and daily decisions.

> *Your success as a couple is found in your daily routines and daily decisions.*

Through our work as chaplains to professional athletes in the NFL, we have learned the importance of muscle memory. Athletes achieve muscle memory through their training and conditioning. They practice repetitive movements and drills repeatedly, so when they are in the game, their bodies and muscles respond automatically. In football, linemen practice coming off the line with correct motions of the hands and feet repeatedly, so their movement becomes second nature. Quarterbacks practice the timing of releasing the football when throwing. Receivers practice running their routes, so their muscles can run, turn, and catch in perfect sync and timing.

A good example of muscle memory is from the movie *The Karate Kid*. Daniel wants to learn karate, so he asks Mr. Miyagi to teach him. However, Mr. Miyagi's unorthodox ways of teaching frustrate Daniel. His training consists of washing and waxing the car, mopping the floor, painting the fence, and completing other household chores, which doesn't make sense to Daniel. To him, these activities don't translate into what he will be doing in his upcoming karate match. But to Daniel's surprise, once Mr. Miyagi tests him, his muscle memory kicks in and he is able to instinctively block punches whenever Mr. Miyagi says, "Wax on" or "Wax off."[3]

Discipline and practice are very important to elite athletes who want to win games. There are no shortcuts to winning; you've got to put the work in if you want to win the game, just as it takes more than love and good looks to stay happily married. As couples, you need discipline and practice to show love and kindness, to have patience, to seek and grant forgiveness, to extend grace, and to exhibit self-control. If you are not practicing these things in the good times, they most likely will not be your automatic response during the difficult seasons of your marriage.

> *Marriage is about progress and growth, not perfection and fairy tales.*

Elite athletes are disciplined about their diets, in addition to training and conditioning their bodies, because they know what they put in their bodies can also influence their performance. What they consume can sabotage their ability to perform at their optimal levels when they are in the game. We all know the saying "Junk in, junk out." When you are under pressure, what you've put in is what comes out. If you fill your head with negativity about your spouse, your relationship, or your circumstances, then when a challenging season comes your way, you may think separation and divorce are the only options. You may believe that your spouse is not what you want or need and that they are to blame for everything, which will not be helpful in winning your home game. Be disciplined about what your mind is consuming daily.

The temptation is to want to take what appears to be the easiest, least taxing way out of the hardships and challenges in your relationship. On the other hand, choosing to put in the hard work pays off big rewards because it produces lasting change instead of temporary fixes. Sometimes people look at a happily married couple and think, *That's what I want*. But they haven't counted the cost of what it took to get there or the daily choices the couple makes to stay there. Have you seen a duck glide easily across a pond? It looks effortless, but the truth is, if you could look under the water, you would see how hard the duck's webbed feet are working. The secret to a great marriage is two people working hard to make it work. We have seen couples who invested time and money to create beautiful and expensive weddings, but when it came time to roll up their sleeves and get to work on their marriage, they didn't put in that same effort and energy. Marriage is about progress and growth, not perfection and fairy tales.

THE PLAYBOOK

Another crucial element needed to win the home game is the playbook. Athletes have their playbook, which contains the plays designed by their coach. Athletes study their playbook religiously and intensely as if their lives depend on it. And they do—not literally their lives but their and their teammates' athletic lives. The players don't make up their own strategies on the field; therefore, they must study and know the plays by heart. The game of football happens at such a fast pace that the players do not have time to go look at the play that is called. They have to know it from memory. This is important because when a play is called, everyone needs to know what is happening and be on the same page so they can run the plays together to succeed.

As couples we, too, need the playbook with the winning strategies given to us by our Coach; we don't need to make up or run our own plays. Our Coach, God, has designed plays to help us succeed in our marriage, and our playbook is the Bible. God created marriage, and He knows what it takes for a couple to succeed.

It has been said that BIBLE is an acronym meaning **B**asic **I**nstructions **B**efore **L**eaving **E**arth. If you have been reading and studying your plays from the Bible, then when tough times hit, you will know what plays to run: when it's time to forgive and what to do when hopelessness and anxiety come against you, when conflicts arise, or when confusion sets in. Remember, a team cannot win if they don't run the same plays together; therefore, a winning strategy must have agreement. You both must agree on a strategy. There is power in agreement because it brings unity and puts you both on the same page, which shields your relationship against confusion and chaos during stressful times.

Even though the Bible is the main source for winning strategies for your relationship, there are additional great coaches that give winning strategies, such as mentors, professional/pastoral counselors, books, conferences, and retreats. Anything we want to excel in requires some type of education, training, or mentorship. When it comes to marriage, most people expect to just excel with little effort or knowledge. However, marriage is one of the most important institutions you will ever be a part of; therefore, it should receive no less education, effort, or training than the other areas you want to succeed in.

When George and I went through a dark season early on in our marriage, instead of doing the same things day in and day out that had had us cycling in the dark for a few years, we agreed to get off the crazy train and do something different. As the saying goes, "Insanity is doing the same thing over and over but expecting a different result." Sometimes couples find themselves caught in unproductive cycles or patterns they know are keeping them stuck, yet they fail to take action to break free. There's a stark contrast between merely complaining about something and actively initiating change. If you find yourselves as a couple experiencing reoccurring cycles or patterns that demand transformation, don't just talk about it—get off the crazy train and take decisive steps to alter your situation or circumstance. If you desire a different outcome, you must be willing to do things differently. In our effort to do something different, George and I decided to attend a marriage conference. I'm not saying the marriage conference was a magic pill, but we learned something new we could work on. We went back to the same conference for seven consecutive years. At each event, we learned and applied something new. It was the small, gradual changes that led us out of the dark place and into helping other couples find their way as well.

What's the message here? Instead of idly waiting for problems to worsen in your relationship, collaborate on a strategy to overcome the obstacles dragging you down. Commit to learning and evolving together within your marriage. When you are going through a tough season in your marriage, it may seem easier to quit and give up, but it's more rewarding to create a game plan and overcome the setbacks and challenges you are facing as a couple.

DEVELOP A WINNING MARRIAGE MINDSET

Knowing the playbook helps with your mindset. When a player knows the playbook, he's more ready and confident to play in the game. The right mindset and attitude are key components of building mental toughness. Resilience is the ability to bounce back from setbacks and maintain a positive outlook even through difficult circumstances.

Each morning you get to choose how you want to respond to life's challenges. Having a winning attitude makes all the difference. Our attitude shapes our beliefs, actions, and desires. A disciplined attitude is one of self-control and delayed gratification. It pushes you to be in control of your emotions despite any given situation. Your response then becomes a question of not what you want to do but what you need to do to achieve your long-term goals. One of our favorite quotes is "Life is 10 percent what happens to you and 90 percent how you react to it."[4] Having the right attitude, along with discipline and practice, empowers you to react in alignment with your goals and win the home game. After all, no one wants their marriage to end in divorce. Both people enter marriage aspiring to cultivate a lasting union.

Having the right mindset helps you win the home game because it gives you the right perspective, and perspective is key. A resilient mindset is a growth mindset that says we will not be defeated; we may get knocked down, but we will get back up again. It's the ability to know you can overcome difficulty. I (Tondra) remember a toy I had as a child. It was a plastic blow-up doll that was weighted on the bottom, and when someone punched it, it would fall back as though it had been knocked out. Every time you knocked it back, it would pop back up. You could not defeat it no matter how hard you hit. This is a great example of resiliency: no matter what obstacles you face, they don't have to defeat you. Just like the plastic inflatable doll, you can bounce back. A resilient mindset thinks, *We can do difficult things. We can overcome.* Sometimes people give up whenever they can't see things getting any better, but God gives us resiliency through hope.

Hope is for the things we cannot see; we don't need hope for what is right before our eyes, for what is tangible and touchable. Hope is about believing there is something higher and greater at work for us. Hope makes you dig deep. That's why we must keep hope alive, so we don't give up. In the Bible, our playbook, Galatians 6:9 encourages us to not lose heart "in doing good, for at the proper time we will reap a harvest if we do not give up."

I can remember one game when the Los Angeles Chargers were playing the Pittsburgh Steelers in Pittsburgh and at halftime the Chargers were losing 23–7. I had given up hope that we could win this game; it seemed impossible for that to happen. But thank God, the team still had hope because when they came back out for the second half, they dug deep and pulled out a win. The Chargers came back and won the game 33–30.[5] No matter where you are or what you're up against, believe, dig deep, and take whatever steps necessary to finish your marriage strong. If something is threatening to destroy your family, don't just stand by and watch it happen. Work hard to stop it.

Coach Anthony Lynn, former head coach of the Chargers, often called this "situational football."[6] By this, he meant finding a way to win at all costs. If something isn't working, then couples also need to find new ways to win. Don't keep doing ineffective things that are not helping you win in your relationship. If you need to find new ways to forgive, new ways to communicate, new ways to budget your finances, new ways of loving each other, new ways of resolving conflict, new ways of seeking help—whatever helps you win, do it. What helped you win in one season might not help you win in another season. Having a winning marriage mindset takes grit (the ability to dig deep), resiliency (belief in your ability to overcome difficulty), and a willingness to grow, learn, and adjust.

REST, RECOVER, REPEAT

Now you may feel a little exhausted after reading the last few sections about discipline, practice, and mindset, so taking a break might sound good about now. Well, you're in luck because another important part of winning the home game is knowing how to rest and recover. Athletes know rest and recovery are just as important as training because rest helps them execute at their optimal level. Rest and recovery help keep their focus and mental game strong; rest keeps them sharp, alert, and energized. As couples, we can learn a lot from this seemingly small sports principle, especially during the stressful seasons of life.

Stress is a normal part of life, as life has ups and downs, which can put pressure on any relationship. We cannot avoid stressful seasons, because they are inevitable. Stress is not all bad; rather, it's how we respond to, think about, and manage it that causes problems. Some people do not embrace, respect, or value rest; others do not know the most effective ways to rest. However, keeping our stress and anxiety levels low when we are in a high-stress stage of life is essential. Managing stress and anxiety during these times enables you to live to fight another day instead of drowning and spinning out of control. Prolonged stress that's not handled well can over time have a negative impact physically, mentally, emotionally, and relationally. It can slowly deteriorate the quality of a couple's relationship and marriage. It reveals the cracks in the foundation of your relationship, which you may have previously been able to ignore and avoid. High levels of stress contribute to more conflict, irritability, impatience, less tolerance, lack of self-control, decrease in sexual desire, isolation, a tendency to blame each other, and overall disconnect with your partner.

So the challenge becomes not letting the stress tear you apart but allowing it to pull you closer together. Remember you are on the same team, and part of being a good teammate is making sure you are taking care of yourself and your relationship. During stressful times you need to give each other individual time to decompress and maintain your well-being. We like to call this "me time." You can't give what you don't have; therefore, pouring into yourself provides you with more to give your spouse—more love, kindness, gentleness, support, and whatever else they need during that stressful season. A relationship can only be as healthy as the two individuals who make it up. You both need time apart from each other to refill and recharge. Time apart does not mean checking out, shutting down, or isolating. "Me time" is scheduled, coordinated, and agreed-upon time apart. And all the introverts say "Amen!"

The extrovert in the relationship must fight the tendency to take their spouse's "me time" personally, as an unloving action, because extroverts may not need or desire alone time. Introverts and extroverts recharge differently. Extroverts draw energy and refreshment from being with others, and introverts draw energy and refreshment from being alone. Their "me time" will look different, and that's okay. An extrovert may prefer going for coffee with friends; however, an introvert may prefer sitting alone reading a book.

Winning the home game takes effort, planning, and execution.

However you choose to spend it, your "me time" is meant to be purposeful. It is not a time to engage in activities that don't recharge you, such as scrolling social media or binge-watching TV. "Me time" is meant for managing stress so you can increase your mental capacity and mental space to cope optimally during your challenges. Electronic devices add to stress levels for many reasons. News content is typically negative. Social media increases FOMO (fear of missing out) and feelings of inadequacy. Electronic devices also emit blue light, which affects the quality of sleep, and they provide access to pornography, which is addictive and destructive.

Sleep is crucial for overall mental and physical health, especially during stressful times. It's not the quantity but the quality of sleep that helps the body restore itself, including decreasing levels of cortisol, which is the stress hormone. The goal of "me time" is to keep the stress levels down. I (Tondra) like to envision stress levels like a water level that rises and falls. When it's high tide, the ocean level moves closer to the shore, making the water level rise, and low tide moves the ocean level farther from the shore, making the water level fall.

If the water levels continue to rise daily without falling, then eventually you will be underwater and drown. This is similar to how stress levels work. If the stress continues to rise daily without falling, then eventually you will be under stress and have difficulty getting your head above water. Managing stress allows your stress level to fall, preventing you from drowning in it. Managing your stress level daily is critical for operating at your peak performance during stressful times.

Understanding you are better together, maintaining mental toughness, and valuing rest and recovery are all necessary to win the home game. Winning the home game takes effort, planning, and execution. You cannot take a back seat and expect to win anything. Implementing tips and strategies from experts who know how to win can help couples develop and execute winning strategies for the home. Teamwork is the key to any winning strategy. Couples need to know they are on the same team. Knowing what team you're on is a critical part of how to win the home game.

Putting It into Practice

QUESTIONS

1. What impacted you most from this chapter, and why?

2. What's one area of your relationship you need to improve to help you win the home game more?

of your emotions despite any given situation. Your response then becomes a question of not what you want to do but what you need to do to achieve your long-term goals. One of our favorite quotes is "Life is 10 percent what happens to you and 90 percent how you react to it."[4] Having the right attitude, along with discipline and practice, empowers you to react in alignment with your goals and win the home game. After all, no one wants their marriage to end in divorce. Both people enter marriage aspiring to cultivate a lasting union.

Having the right mindset helps you win the home game because it gives you the right perspective, and perspective is key. A resilient mindset is a growth mindset that says we will not be defeated; we may get knocked down, but we will get back up again. It's the ability to know you can overcome difficulty. I (Tondra) remember a toy I had as a child. It was a plastic blow-up doll that was weighted on the bottom, and when someone punched it, it would fall back as though it had been knocked out. Every time you knocked it back, it would pop back up. You could not defeat it no matter how hard you hit. This is a great example of resiliency: no matter what obstacles you face, they don't have to defeat you. Just like the plastic inflatable doll, you can bounce back. A resilient mindset thinks, *We can do difficult things. We can overcome.* Sometimes people give up whenever they can't see things getting any better, but God gives us resiliency through hope.

Hope is for the things we cannot see; we don't need hope for what is right before our eyes, for what is tangible and touchable. Hope is about believing there is something higher and greater at work for us. Hope makes you dig deep. That's why we must keep hope alive, so we don't give up. In the Bible, our playbook, Galatians 6:9 encourages us to not lose heart "in doing good, for at the proper time we will reap a harvest if we do not give up."

I can remember one game when the Los Angeles Chargers were playing the Pittsburgh Steelers in Pittsburgh and at halftime the Chargers were losing 23–7. I had given up hope that we could win this game; it seemed impossible for that to happen. But thank God, the team still had hope because when they came back out for the second half, they dug deep and pulled out a win. The Chargers came back and won the game 33–30.[5] No matter where you are or what you're up against, believe, dig deep, and take whatever steps necessary to finish your marriage strong. If something is threatening to destroy your family, don't just stand by and watch it happen. Work hard to stop it.

Coach Anthony Lynn, former head coach of the Chargers, often called this "situational football."[6] By this, he meant finding a way to win at all costs. If something isn't working, then couples also need to find new ways to win. Don't keep doing ineffective things that are not helping you win in your relationship. If you need to find new ways to forgive, new ways to communicate, new ways to budget your finances, new ways of loving each other, new ways of resolving conflict, new ways of seeking help—whatever helps you win, do it. What helped you win in one season might not help you win in another season. Having a winning marriage mindset takes grit (the ability to dig deep), resiliency (belief in your ability to overcome difficulty), and a willingness to grow, learn, and adjust.

REST, RECOVER, REPEAT

Now you may feel a little exhausted after reading the last few sections about discipline, practice, and mindset, so taking a break might sound good about now. Well, you're in luck because another important part of winning the home game is knowing how to rest and recover. Athletes know rest and recovery are just as important as training because rest helps them execute at their optimal level. Rest and recovery help keep their focus and mental game strong; rest keeps them sharp, alert, and energized. As couples, we can learn a lot from this seemingly small sports principle, especially during the stressful seasons of life.

Stress is a normal part of life, as life has ups and downs, which can put pressure on any relationship. We cannot avoid stressful seasons, because they are inevitable. Stress is not all bad; rather, it's how we respond to, think about, and manage it that causes problems. Some people do not embrace, respect, or value rest; others do not know the most effective ways to rest. However, keeping our stress and anxiety levels low when we are in a high-stress stage of life is essential. Managing stress and anxiety during these times enables you to live to fight another day instead of drowning and spinning out of control. Prolonged stress that's not handled well can over time have a negative impact physically, mentally, emotionally, and relationally. It can slowly deteriorate the quality of a couple's relationship and marriage. It reveals the cracks in the foundation of your relationship, which you may have previously been able to ignore and avoid. High levels of stress contribute to more conflict, irritability, impatience, less tolerance, lack of self-control, decrease in sexual desire, isolation, a tendency to blame each other, and overall disconnect with your partner.

So the challenge becomes not letting the stress tear you apart but allowing it to pull you closer together. Remember you are on the same team, and part of being a good teammate is making sure you are taking care of yourself and your relationship. During stressful times you need to

3. What is your current mindset during challenging times in your relationship? What changes do you need to make to gain a winning mindset?

4. In what areas do you need to be more disciplined about creating muscle memory in your relationship (forgiveness, grace, self-control, etc.)? What's one small step you can take toward that new habit?

5. What steps can be taken to make practicing rest and recovery more of a priority in your home?

COUPLE'S ACTIVITY: SET RELATIONSHIP GOALS

Goals are the desired result you and your spouse are committed to achieving. Relationship declarations are concise, affirming statements that articulate specific goals in their fully realized form.[7]

Goals need to be SMART ...	*Relationship declarations need to be ...*
Specific	Positive
Measurable	Affirming
Attainable	Empowering
Relevant	Spoken daily
Time-bound[8]	

1. Write three goals you want to accomplish as a couple to win your home game in every season of marriage. Example of a SMART goal: "We will deepen our friendship by having connection conversations weekly for at least one hour and participating in one shared experience per month starting this Saturday." (This is instead of the general goal to spend more time together.)

2. Write a relationship declaration for each goal (listed in number 1) to motivate and inspire a winning mindset. For example: "We share a profound love for each other and delight in each other's company."

3. Find and list two or three Scripture verses from God's playbook (the Bible) to stand on for strength and encouragement when you face challenging seasons as a couple.

4. What obstacles or challenges will you face in trying to accomplish your goals, and how will you overcome them?

PRAYER POINTS TO CONSIDER

ACTION ITEMS
(What steps, actions, or decisions do you need to make or take?)

TIME-OUT
For further insights and practical tips from this chapter, take a time-out and view our short bonus video, "Time-Out: Winning the Home Game," using this link or QR code:

https://davidccook.org/access
Access code: GamePlan

Chapter 4

WE ARE ON THE SAME TEAM

The only way to win is as a team.

Pelé

Coming together is a beginning, keeping together is progress, working together is success.

Henry Ford

In 1992 the US men's basketball team won Olympic gold. They will forever be known as the Dream Team. The Dream Team consisted of a historic star-studded list of athletes, including Michael Jordan, Magic Johnson, Larry Bird, Patrick Ewing, Charles Barkley, Scottie Pippen, John Stockton, Karl Malone, Chris Mullin, David Robinson, Clyde Drexler, and Christian Laettner. To win the gold, the Dream Team had to come together and put aside their personalities, differences, and individual team jerseys. It is indeed true: teamwork makes the dream work.

A sports team is composed of individuals who collectively come together to amass their athletic talents, determination, creativity, and passion to win. While each individual is talented and passionate, the goal is to come together as a team to accomplish something that one individual cannot do alone. On a team, you experience the joys of glorious wins and the pain of agonizing defeats.

The same is true of the marriage team. When a couple comes together, it is critically important to gel together as a team. Sure, both spouses come from different backgrounds, families, and cultures, but for the sake of winning in life together, each spouse must check their individual jerseys at the door and become one new team. If couples are going to win gold in their marriage as a dream team, they must learn to play, sacrifice, and build together.

One of the greatest images that captures a team working together in harmony to accomplish a task is that of a married couple. When two people get married, they become one new team. Marriage is not an individual activity. Marriage is about two distinct individuals being joined together. When Tondra and I got married, we became one new team—Team Gregory. The same is true for you and your spouse. You are on the same team. Now might be a good opportunity to grab your spouse by the hand and declare, "We are on the same team!"

> *When two people get married, they become one new team.*

WE ALL WANT TO BE PART OF A WINNING TEAM

Very few people sign up to be on a team simply because they want to play or love the sport. Anyone who plays sports wants to be a part of the winner's circle. I (George) don't know anyone who has signed up to be on a losing team. That simply does not happen, because it goes against the reason real athletes play the game. Teams play to win. The desire to win should be no different on a team in marriage. To win, teams must possess a winning mentality like Coach Prime Time himself, Deion Sanders. During one of his hype sessions with his teams, Sanders said, "I don't know if y'all know it, but we are going to win. I don't know if you feel it, but we are going to win.

I don't know if you can see it, but we are going to win. You got to understand we are going to win right now. Not later. Right now."[1]

No matter what you think of Coach Sanders, we should all take note of this winning attitude from the start of our marriage or during our marriage preparation process. Couples who come together on the same team must have a winning mindset and not be content with simply being married. Daily we must wake up and approach the challenges or strains within our marital relationship with hope, determination, and a mindset that we are going to win. In fact, we need to huddle up with our spouse daily or weekly and reassure each other that we are going to win against any problem, attitude, season, or opponent that comes against our marriage and family.

Two passionate and committed people who say "I do" and choose to build a life together on a new team can win in marriage with the right mindset and approach. In doing thousands of premarital counseling sessions and officiating the weddings of hundreds of couples, I (George) have not met one couple who signed up to lose or fail in their marriage—not one. Most, if not all, start out thinking they will win in their marriage against all odds.

WINNING AGAINST ALL ODDS

Marriage is a team sport designed by God for two people to come together and forsake all others. A marriage covenant is best played or lived out together—in unity and partnership, working as a team to win no matter the odds. It takes two willing people to make a marriage work. But just like all sports teams, no matter how much we desire to be on the same team to win, there might be some seasons in a marriage where we feel as if we've fallen behind or are on the brink of a losing season. Going through tough seasons on any team is not easy. Not winning will affect the teamwork and chemistry of a team. If this describes your marriage season right now, we want to encourage you that you can make it out of this season or slump. You can bounce back if you are willing to go all in and prepare for a comeback. We all like great comeback stories.

Some of the most memorable sports games in history are those where teams have been counted out and written off but somehow found the determination, passion, and togetherness to come back against all odds to win together. Here are some examples of great comebacks in sports:

- "The Comeback"—The 1993 AFC (American Football Conference) Wild Card game between the Houston Oilers and the Buffalo Bills. Despite the Buffalo Bills being down 35–3 in the third quarter, the Bills found a way to fight back and win in overtime, 41–38.[2]
- "Baseball's Greatest Miracle"—In 2004 the Boston Red Sox defeated the New York Yankees in the World Series. After losing the first three games to the Yankees, the Red Sox became the first team in Major League history to come back from a three-game deficit in the World Series, defeating the Yankees in seven games.[3]
- "Greatest Comeback in Sports"—In Super Bowl LI the New England Patriots trailed the Atlanta Falcons by 25 points in the third quarter. The Patriots never gave up and fought back to win in overtime, 34–28.[4]
- "The Miracle Minute"—In 2001 the Duke Blue Devils trailed the Maryland Terrapins 90–80 with one minute to play in the game. Duke fought back to win 98–96.[5]
- "The Greatest NBA Comeback"—In 1996 the Utah Jazz came back from a 36-point deficit to win over the Denver Nuggets. At halftime the score was 70–36. The final score was 107–103.[6]

This is just a sample of great comebacks in sports. Everyone loves a great comeback. Seeing sports teams that are down and out find a way to rally together and win makes great stories and memories. But great comebacks are not just for sports teams. Great comebacks can and do happen in marriage. To have a great comeback, couples, just like sports teams, must find a way to win and beat the odds.

Couples can't come back from setbacks if they are not willing to go all in and do whatever it takes to win. Great comebacks are not achievable without making great sacrifices and fighting through moments of pain and discouragement. Marriage teams can come back when they remember and fight for what they started out desiring in the first place—to win together! The mentality to fight for and win in your marriage cannot happen without both partners being all in and being guardians of victory. As Coach Jim Harbaugh, head coach of the Los Angeles Chargers, once said, "Being the guardian of victory is probably the number-one job you have. Making sure that the decisions you're making are complementary on all three phases. There's no offense. There's no defense. It's a we-fense."[7] Winning in your marriage will take both spouses fighting for a strong "we-fense" no matter where you are on your journey.

Whether your marriage needs a great comeback or you are reading this book simply to help you out along your marriage journey, I encourage you to take a shot at preparing a game plan for your marriage and relationship. The great National Hockey League prince Wayne Gretzky recalls his coaches saying, "You miss 100 percent of the shots you never take."[8] Now is the time to take the shot at winning together with a solid game plan.

You can bounce back if you are willing to go all in and prepare for a comeback.

YOU ARE NOT MY ENEMY

Sometimes in marriage, although we are on the same team, it can feel as if we are enemies or on opposing teams, especially during moments when we are clearly not on the same page, have unresolved conflict, or cannot see eye to eye. Over the last thirty years of being married, we have gotten into a few heated conversations that were not as productive and team oriented as we had hoped. We call these moments "intense fellowship." During intense fellowship, we do not feel like we are on the same team.

But the opposite is true. We are and always will be on the same team. Since we are on the same team, one thing should be very clear: Even during a disagreement, miscommunication, and intensity, we are not enemies. We are on the same team 365 good and bad days of the year.

One day, after a heated exchange, we were reminded by reading a familiar passage in Ephesians that we were not enemies. Rather, we were fighting against a common enemy that sought to kill, steal, and destroy the love that we had grown and developed (John 10:10). Ephesians 6:10–12 made it clear who our real Enemy was:

> Finally, be strong in the Lord and in his mighty power. Put on the full armor of God, so that you can take your stand against the devil's schemes. For our struggle is not against flesh and blood, but against the rulers, against the authorities, against the powers of this dark world and against the spiritual forces of evil in the heavenly realms.

As Christians, we, like most couples, needed to identify that the Enemy of our souls (the Devil) was out to destroy everything that we worked so hard at building together as teammates. His main task was to make us both feel as though we were each other's opponent or enemy. In the next chapter, we will dig deeper and discuss the enemies of our past, soul, and mind that come against our marriages. But in this section, we wanted to start with how at times couples can feel like their spouse is the actual enemy.

In reading Ephesians 6:10–12, all couples should realize that our struggle is not against our spouse ("flesh and blood") but against an opponent and enemy that does not fight fairly or play according to the rules. Instead, many times we are really fighting "against the spiritual forces of evil in the heavenly realms" or high places. We call this spiritual warfare. At times you might think you are fighting against or at odds with your spouse, but it is really "the rulers" and "the authorities" and "the powers of this dark world" attempting to cause division and prevent teamwork. The Devil comes against our marriages and families with supernatural schemes and plans to destroy and dismantle our marriage covenant and vows.

As a result of this Scripture, we have a unique code phrase in our marriage that we often verbalize when we feel like enemies due to our tone or moments of intense fellowship. We have taught thousands of couples around the world this powerful code phrase wherever we speak. That unique phrase is simple—*You are not my enemy!* It is intended to be an alert that the Devil's schemes, although real, can be detected. Once we sense there is something at work in our relationship to destroy our oneness, unity, and teamwork, we declare, "You are not my enemy." This helps redirect us from fighting each other to going after the real Enemy. Each spouse has to allow the code phrase to reorient them in order for it to help. The goal in marriage is to fight for unity, not against each other.

Imagine if every married couple could discern and identify when the Devil is sending his A-team to defeat our marriages and destroy our families. What if couples realized and sensed when spiritual forces in high places were intent on keeping them arguing with each other instead of fighting the real Enemy, who seeks to destroy the family and foundation of society? Make no mistake about it, the Devil wants you to feel and think that your spouse is your enemy, and he will do everything to manipulate you and discourage you from working together as a team. But you must declare, "You are not my enemy," anytime you feel division or discord in your marriage.

But note the Devil is not responsible for all the problems that come up in marriages. Certainly, we know that spouses can do things to cause division and break down God's plan for oneness, unity, and teamwork. Things such as infidelity, pride, hardened hearts, anger, and the inability to communicate or resolve conflict cannot be overlooked and oversimplified as "it's just the Devil's fault." Husbands and wives need to admit when they are the doer of the deed. Each of us must own the things that we bring into and allow to stay in our marriages.

And yet if you are a Christian, the Bible clearly tells us the Devil's role in this world and one of his overarching assignments is to bring division and distractions, especially against the covenant of marriage. Throughout the Bible, he is clearly described as an adversary, destroyer, enemy, tempter, accuser of the brethren, and the list goes on and on. He fights against God's original plan for oneness and teamwork.

As couples, we must be vigilant in discerning his schemes, plans, and presence in our marriages. I remember one day on our way to church we were having a spirited disagreement. (Don't judge us, but some of our best moments of intense fellowship have been on our way to church.) We were both going back and forth attempting to win the argument.

Suddenly, I (George) remembered the passage in Ephesians 6:10–12, and I said, "Tondra, I believe the Devil is laughing at both of us right now as he wants us to continue arguing and not seeing eye to eye." In a very humble voice, I asked her, "Can we please say a prayer together and kick the Devil out of our car?"

Tondra, however, was not having it, because she wanted to get in one last point!

I said, "Baby, so you want the Devil to keep riding with us and causing disagreement?"

She said, "Um-hum … he's feeling real good right now!" The moral of this story is to not let the Devil ride too long!

Perhaps now is a good place to simply pause and pray and expose the true Enemy of all relationships. Pause for a moment and resist blaming your spouse for everything that is going wrong and simply pray this prayer:

> Lord, I want to confess the things that I've brought into our marriage and the things that I've allowed to stay there. [Simply confess them out loud one by one.] I also acknowledge that You have brought me and my spouse together to become one and work together as a team. I declare that my spouse is not my enemy and that we are on the same team. I say no to any of the Devil's plans and assignments to make me feel as if my spouse is my enemy. I say no to his accusations, temptations, and plans to destroy what You have brought together. In Jesus' name. Amen.

MARRIAGE IS A COVENANT, NOT A CONTRACT

Often when a spouse is viewed as an enemy or an antagonist in the relationship, marriage can be seen more like a contract than a covenant. At this point, couples can lose sight of the goal. Being on the same team in marriage is about living out a covenant, not living under a contract. During wedding ceremonies, there is always a time for the bride and groom to exchange wedding vows. As we wrote in chapter 2 ("The Playbook on Marriage"), vows are essentially promises or covenants that couples express to each other. These covenants are based on lifelong commitments and are never spoken of as temporal promises that may change over time based on circumstances.

The confirmation of these covenants during the wedding ceremony is confirmed with the solemn promise "until death do us part." The essential meaning of the covenant promise is you can count on me as your teammate in any circumstance until we are separated only by death. Although these are covenants until death, many couples treat these vows as temporal promises, which makes marriage look and feel more like a contract than a covenant relationship.

A contract is about protecting ourselves and our interests. It's easily voided when one party can no longer get what they want or bargained for. A contract view of marriage can lead a spouse to create a plan B and invest little effort to fight for their marriage. Often contract marriages are based on our ideas about what marriage should do for us as individuals.

A covenant view of marriage is just the opposite. It is based on unconditional love, loyalty, and commitment for life. It is about growing together through good and bad times and becoming one. A covenant view of marriage is not based on our own ideas; it is based on God's idea of and plan for marriage. How we view marriage—as a covenant or contract—is vitally important.

In our culture, marriage has been so watered down that many couples believe it's easier to start over than to believe God can reconcile, restore, and renew a marriage. Today, marriage covenants can be dissolved without much hassle or consideration. While we were living in New York City for ten years, we were bombarded with images and billboards that not only encouraged ending marriage covenants but also highlighted how cheap and easy it was to get divorced.

One billboard read, "Divorce $399. Spouse's signature not needed." Another said, "Cheap divorces. Buy one divorce, get the next one half off. End the misery today." And we will never forget six months of daily being given free newspapers before boarding NYC subways with the infamous Ashley Madison slogan printed on the entire back, "Life is short. Have an affair." All these signs and slogans point to the reality that we live in a historic time when there is enormous confusion about marriage being a contract rather than a covenant.

ACCEPTING YOUR SPOUSE'S DIFFERENCES

One of the biggest challenges that couples face in marriage is their differences.

Becoming one and being on the same team requires a lot of hard work and sacrifice. A sports team is made up of different individuals who bring different personalities, strengths, and skills to the team. For example, football teams consist of players who play in different phases of the game—offense, defense, and special teams. Each phase has players playing different roles and bringing a different set of skills and strengths to the gameplay. Some players block, tackle, and try to sack the quarterback. Others try to throw, run, kick, and catch the ball to advance down the field. Not every player brings the same things to the game of football.

Marriage is no different. A marriage, just like a sports team, is made up of different individuals who bring different personalities, strengths, gifts, and resources to the team. Differences in marriage between spouses help maintain balance and a true sense of partnership. Having differences often feels like you are pulling in two different directions, but, in reality, you are strengthening your output and becoming more well-rounded as a team. Instead of allowing your differences to pull you apart, explore how your differences help make you a stronger team and cohesive unit. Embrace how you are different instead of allowing your differences to divide you.

Your spouse will most likely be stronger in an area that you may not be as strong in. This helps the team. It does not detract from the team. We are stronger together than we are apart. Differences can pull us apart, but the key is allowing them to bring us together, what we call "filling each other's gaps." In the movie *Rocky*, the character Rocky, thinking about how he and Adrian made a good team together relationally, said, "She's got gaps. I got gaps. Together, we fill gaps."[9] In your marriage, you have gaps, and your spouse has gaps. However, together you help fill each other's gaps. What a great picture of a marriage team!

In the first few years of our married life together, we certainly found out that we both had gaps that needed filling. For me (George), I needed someone to help me stop and smell the roses. I was a type-A, task-oriented guy who prided himself on getting the job done by any means necessary. This often meant working late nights and not taking time off for myself or the family. I was on my way to becoming the world's greatest workaholic. I am sure there are many reading this who can relate.

Tondra is wired much differently than I am; she is just the opposite. She is not type A in the least. Tondra prided herself on being the opposite of me, as she loved to live in the gray. She wanted to be present in every part of life and enjoy the simplest of moments by creating memories. Tondra was the one who scheduled vacations and could remember every word that each of us said. She was indeed the nurturer because nurturing takes time, and all calendars and outside projects were secondary to her role as nurturer.

Now these differences seem rather innocent and unharmful, but within the first two years of our marriage, our differences had each of us quoting the title of Tyler Perry's movie—*Why Did I Get Married?*—ten years before it was made. Being type A, I was a stickler for being on time. And not just on time, but early, because my father had taught me that being on time was being fifteen minutes early. Tondra, however, was raised with the sentiment that everyone is given the grace to be fifteen minutes fashionably late. Can you feel my pain? We inevitably clashed in how we both viewed "time." To me, being fifteen minutes fashionably late meant that you were not respecting someone else's time. It was a value that had been instilled in me but was now being challenged by my wife and teammate.

Over the years, instead of fighting each other regarding our differences, we had to see how our differences made us better so they would not pull us apart. Tondra's love of living in the gray worked wonders for me in some areas, but it rubbed me the wrong way in others. Her approach positively shaped me in two ways: it helped me learn to slow down and to enjoy making memories in the moment. Tondra showed me that not every day and minute had to be set aside to accomplish a goal or tick something off my endless to-do list. Once I started to embrace her differences as something good, she in turn saw how my different wiring helped her as well.

Now Tondra has a calendar and smartphone and keeps up with tasks that she needs to accomplish. My type-A wiring taught her how to set goals and achieve things in a timely manner, which brings a sense of accomplishment and purpose. As she leaned into allowing my different personality to shape her, Tondra set a goal of getting her master's in mental health counseling and started a thriving counseling practice in the heart of NYC's Times Square. Now that's teamwork at its best!

I know many of you are wondering how our big difference in viewing time affected us in getting to places together on time. We are happy to report we did not allow our differences to break us apart or continue fighting each other for years. Instead, we had to learn a key word—*compromise*. In marriage, neither spouse gets to have it their way 100 percent of the time. We must find a way to compromise and find common ground.

In your marriage or relationship, you don't have to allow differences to cause division or ruin your love for each other. Instead, you can use your differences to draw closer together by finding a way to view them as an asset rather than a liability. Another way of saying this is, find a way to see your spouse's differences as a needed strength that will help fill your gaps. Most spouses are opposite in some respect. There are always differences in spending versus saving, getting up early versus staying up late, having a quick response for everything or waiting for a well-thought-out answer, and so on. We are different as people, but together our differences should make us better and more well-rounded as a team instead of weighing us down.

SELFISHNESS CAN DESTROY A MARRIAGE

Being on the same team and growing at perfecting teamwork is not just a good idea; it's a God idea. From the beginning of time, God wired and shaped us to not walk alone. God knew if we tried to walk alone, we would be perfectly imperfect. Like Adam and Eve, we all need someone to help fill our gaps as a companion and partner. Through our union in marriage, God brings two perfectly imperfect people together to complete and complement each other as a team.

Being on the same team is God's simple reminder that we, as married couples, are better together when we choose oneness. As teammates on the same team, we each bring to our sacred unions the divine ability to be a "helper." As mentioned before, as spouses, we are designed to help each other succeed and not fall. Together we fight our enemies, not each other. Our divine call is to help each other win and conquer as one.

We'd like to offer a subjective and more personal way that we have read and inserted our names in Ecclesiastes 4:9–10, 12. We call this the Journey for Life Version as it has become our key verse over the course of our marriage. The version below is how I read the text as a reminder that I need Tondra as a spouse and helper:

> Tondra and I are better off than I am by myself, because Tondra and I help each other succeed. If I fall, Tondra is there to reach out and help me. But when I fall alone, I am in real trouble. Standing alone, I can be attacked and defeated, but Tondra and I can stand back to back and conquer.

For more than thirty years, we've read this Scripture and inserted our names when we've hit our rough spots, as all couples inevitably do. It's in the rough spots that we all tend to think we are better off by ourselves, and that simply is not true. It's a major issue in our contemporary society to just want to hit the eject button rather than ask for God's redemptive touch in our marriage when things get tough.

Teamwork is essentially about a collective group of individuals coming together with different gifts and talents in order to win. NBA teams continually relearn this truth: "Five guys on the court working together can achieve more than five talented individuals who come and go as individuals." In marriage, two people coming together can achieve more than two selfish individuals who cannot work together. Togetherness makes the team gel as one, while selfishness ultimately sabotages a team.

During the first few years of our marriage, I found it hard to let go of my selfish tendencies. As a single person, I thought my way of doing things and seeing the world was the way everyone did and saw things. The only problem—I was no longer single. I was married to Tondra, who did not see or do things the way I did. She did not see the world through my narrow lens.

To go a step further, I entered my marriage thinking I was right about everything and that I brought a lot more to the table than Tondra did based on our different upbringings. I entered my marriage with a selfish perspective. I thought if I could just "fix" her, our marriage problems would suddenly cease. I thought it was my role to help her see how to do marriage properly because I came from a two-parent household. Boy, was I wrong! Although I was married, I was still thinking much like a single man who knew it all and could help my wife if she would only let me.

> It's a major issue in our contemporary society to just want to hit the eject button rather than ask for God's redemptive touch in our marriage when things get tough.

Many of our conversations early in our marriage were about how she could improve in an area or how much we needed to change something around the household. I must admit, my selfishness caused a lot of our moments of intense fellowship. Tondra was fighting to be on the same team while I was selfishly jockeying to be the captain and the hero of the team. I was the loud and vocal one, while she was more of a processor and not as verbal. That is, until one day she spoke with power and passion and asked me, "Do you know what I bring to this marriage?"

I pondered for a second and selfishly said, "I'm not sure. Let me get back to you."

That answer was certainly not the right answer; it only pointed to the growth that I desperately needed.

Never has a question shaken me to my core like that one did. It was as if she reached into my soul and turned a light on. I had been blind to the way I was treating her and not valuing what she brought to our marriage. I mean, I could easily rattle off a few things that she brought to our marriage, but the question made me finally understand how she felt. The issue was not what I would say in response to her question but how I would respond to her heart. Instead of making her feel unheard and devalued as a wife and partner, my answer to her question was to show her she was valuable through my words and actions.

That day we became a stronger team and were finally on the path to becoming one. Marriage is about two becoming one. Two imperfect people being joined together by God and vowing to love and cherish each other for life. The key word here is *together*. Becoming one and being on the same team creates oneness and solidarity. The opposite of oneness in marriage is individualism, which ultimately leads to isolation. Oneness drives us toward each other, while individualism drives us away from each other until one or both spouses feel isolated and alone. We all get married to come together on a new team and experience something wonderful together. No one desires to be married and feel alone. Yet selfishness and self-centered ways can destroy any team and marriage.

Instead of allowing selfishness to destroy our marriages, we must be willing to make the necessary sacrifices for the sake of our spouse and team. Pittsburgh Steelers coach Mike Tomlin said it best when he said, "It's not what you [are] capable of. It's what you [are] willing to do. I know plenty of people that are capable. I know fewer people that are willing…. Will is a powerful thing. Ask yourself, what are you willing to do?"[10] Are you willing to do whatever it takes to win in your marriage?

Putting It into Practice

QUESTIONS

1. What impacted you most from this chapter, and why?

2. What are some ways you and your spouse are alike and different?

Ways You Are Alike	Ways You Are Different

3. How can the ways you are different from your spouse make you stronger in your marriage? What makes this challenging?

4. What steps can you take to ensure you remain on the same team throughout your marriage?

5. What are the things that make you feel like your spouse is your enemy at times in your marriage?

6. What is at least one thing you can work on as a team to accomplish in your marriage during this season?

COUPLE'S ACTIVITY: WORKING AS A TEAM

1. Come up with a unique code phrase to employ when you feel like enemies and tensions are rising. This code will serve as a gentle reminder that, despite disagreements, you are on the same team working toward common goals. For example, our unique code phrase is "You are not my enemy."

2. Schedule regular "team huddles" during the week to foster connection and unity. Dedicate one or two specific times each week to come together and engage in activities to deepen your bond, such as uplifting each other, addressing relationship needs, or simply sharing updates.

Time(s):

3. On a computer, type out the Journey for Life Version of Ecclesiastes 4:9–10, 12, provided for you below. As we stated in this chapter, it has become our key verse over the course of our marriage. Remember to personalize the Scripture by inserting your spouse's name in the blanks. Consider printing out and placing the Scripture passage in your home in an area that you tend to run to the most when times get rough. It can be a reminder that you and your spouse are united in purpose, striving to support and uplift each other toward success and victory.

_____ and I are better off than I am by myself, because _____ and I help each other succeed. If I fall, _____ is there to reach out and help me. But when I fall alone, I am in real trouble. Standing alone, I can be attacked and defeated, but _____ and I can stand back to back and conquer.

PRAYER POINTS TO CONSIDER

ACTION ITEMS
(What steps, actions, or decisions do you need to make or take?)

TIME-OUT

For further insights and practical tips from this chapter, take a time-out and view our short bonus video, "Time-Out: We Are on the Same Team," using this link or QR code:

https://davidccook.org/access

Access code: GamePlan

Chapter 5

FACING AND OVERCOMING YOUR OPPONENTS

It isn't the mountains ahead to climb that wear you out; it's the pebble in your shoe.
Muhammad Ali

The game of football has made studying opponents a complete art and science. When we began working with professional football teams in the NFL, we were truly amazed at how critical knowing your opponents is to a game-winning strategy. One player said it like this, "My job is to study one man all week." His goal is to know whichever opponent he is up against that week inside and out, to know that player's strengths and weakness so he can anticipate his opponent's every move to overcome him. No championship team is crowned without defeating opponents along the way. Overcoming opponents is simply a part of the game.

Like sports teams, spouses have opponents that must be overcome. There are numerous obstacles coming to divide you and your spouse, to prevent you from being unified and on the same team. We call these obstacles "opponents." The goal of your opponent is to expose and exploit your weaknesses to stop you from winning. Therefore, you must know who your opponents are and how they're coming against you.

Here are some opponents to a healthy marriage. Identify and circle the opponents you are facing.

selfishness	disrespect	hostility
infidelity	isolation	unhealthy communication
criticism	resentment	parenting
unforgiveness	bitterness	health issues
in-laws	divorce	finances
sex/intimacy	pride	unresolved conflict
careers	blame	fertility issues
boredom		

As couples, you must know the opponents that have the potential to try your marital bond. You cannot be clueless or in denial that external combatants of marital oneness have the propensity to come out of nowhere at any given moment or opportunity. In addition, you must be open and honest with each other about the opponents within your marriage that are seeking to wreak havoc. Once you identify any current opponents, you must create a safe place to discuss a game plan to come together as a team and defeat anything that comes against your marital union. In addition to external opponents, we also face internal opponents, such as our past, soul, and mind. In some cases, you know specifically what these opponents are; however, some of them are unconscious and outside your awareness. Uncovering what internal opponents you face gives you a better chance to fight against and overcome them.

ENEMY OF YOUR PAST

One big internal opponent you must overcome in marriage is your past. It's a powerful lens that shapes and filters how you view your relationship, your spouse, and yourself. The past could cause you to see things in a skewed and distorted way. Unresolved baggage could cause you to be less objective and more reactive in your relationship. It is crucial to clear the lens. You are married to a lot more than your eyes can see. Your spouse brings with them experiences, beliefs, and expectations to your relationship and marriage. No matter how "perfect" or "imperfect" of a family you grew up in, we all bring baggage, and most of us have no idea what's in our bags or how our baggage will interact with our spouse's.

When I (Tondra) travel, the most stressful thing is packing and carrying the luggage. Sometimes I overpack because I'm trying to predict what I will need for the journey and I'm afraid to need it and not have it. Oftentimes when George picks up my bags he says, "Girl, what in the world did you pack?" Carrying and keeping up with heavy, excess baggage can be exhausting. It really weighs me down, and when I arrive at my destination, I realize I don't need most of the things I packed. Packing unnecessary items often prevents me from making room for the things I do need, such as a toothbrush, suit jacket, laptop, or my shoes or medication.

As couples, you need to ask yourself these questions: What are you packing and carrying from your past that's weighing you and your relationship down, causing you unnecessary stress and frustration? What's preventing you from having the things you need to be successful in your marriage journey? Maybe your baggage is from a previous romantic relationship or from your relationship with your parents or siblings. Baggage can stem from a boss or from work experience, school experience, lifestyle choices, poor decisions, or trauma. Most people believe the past is the past and has nothing to do with the present or the future. This could not be further from the truth.

The past remains in your brain, stored away until something activates or triggers it. You are powerless to change your past if you ignore it and refuse to deal with it. You can have power over your past and truly move beyond it only by processing and understanding it, which will enable you to make peace with it, let it go, and move on. The danger in not dealing with your baggage is that the unresolved issues from the past have a way of repeating themselves.

For example, if your father used alcohol to numb himself from feeling pain, his addiction may have caused him to neglect and abuse you. Then, to protect yourself from the pain caused by your father, you became angry and bitter. The anger and bitterness hardened your heart to numb you from feeling pain. Once you have a child, that child will experience the same feelings of neglect and abuse because of your walls, which causes disconnection. This is the same disconnection you felt from the wall created by your father's alcoholism. Hurt people hurt people. These destructive patterns are the types of things that get uncovered in premarital and marital counseling. The goal is to catch destructive patterns before couples settle into them and keep the cycle going.

The past shapes you in ways you rarely understand unless you uncover the hidden, buried baggage that threatens to poison your relationship and the new family you are trying to build. Rather than downplaying its significance, you must acknowledge and plan for the impact of your past experiences. George and I were unaware of how our respective upbringings would shape the foundation of our marriage. While George was raised in a traditional two-parent household with his father as the dominant figure and his mother taking a more submissive role, I grew up in a single-parent household where my mother held the dominant position. Consequently, I lacked exposure to the dynamics of husband-wife interactions and cooperation.

> *You are married to a lot more than your eyes can see.*

Entering marriage, we found ourselves on different pages regarding leadership and collaboration. George naturally assumed the role of leading our home, while I also sought to assert control, resulting in an unseen power struggle. Hindsight has made it clear that we were caught in this subconscious conflict without realizing it until we uncovered how our past baggage was impacting our present relationship.

Some more of the baggage George and I packed from our past that threatened our marriage was how the families we grew up in handled communication. George grew up in a family where they could say what they were thinking in very direct ways to each other with the expectation that no one should be offended or hurt by what was said. This led George to lack tact when communicating. I grew up in a family where words were used to punish and control. This caused me to take words as a personal attack, leading me to feel pressured to avoid mistakes because those mistakes meant I wasn't good enough.

This dynamic created repeated miscommunication and conflict in our relationship. I would feel personally attacked by anything George said about improvements or his needs. George felt frustrated because he didn't know what to say or how to say things authentically without upsetting me. George would also dismiss my feelings of being hurt by his wording because he thought I was being too sensitive. He would tell me, "Stop wearing your heart on your sleeve." This was our perpetual pattern of poor communication and led to gridlock where each of us felt the other was wrong and unreasonable. Most of the time our conflicts were left without resolve. Often, we would argue until one of us was too worn out to continue defending ourselves.

Another piece of baggage I brought into our marriage was a huge mistrust of men. As mentioned in previous chapters, I was raised by independent women who had been let down, abandoned, and betrayed by every man in their lives. To prevent me from suffering the same hurt and disappointment, they raised me to not trust or have any expectations of men because all they were going to do was disappoint me and cause me pain. My mother and grandmother instilled in me beliefs such as "Never put all your eggs in one basket," "Always have a plan B," and "It's not *if* a man will let you down, but it's *when* he lets you down. You have to be ready." My level of trust in and expectation for men in general, but especially my husband, were very low.

The mistrust I brought in from my past caused me to believe my marriage would not work. Therefore, instead of working on my marriage, I was watching and waiting for the marriage and George to fail me. Instead of giving my best effort and sacrificing, I was working on protecting myself from being hurt when it didn't work out. I was just looking and waiting for George to give me a reason to call it quits. I struggled with a strong sense of independence and self-sufficiency. I took too much pride in my ability to do things on my own, not needing any help.

George, on the other hand, had baggage from his past romantic escapades with women. George was a "fraternity boy" with a huge ego. He was a womanizer and ladies' man. He thought he was God's gift to women. For him, it was a scary thought to be with only one woman for the rest of his life. He questioned whether he could be faithful.

Thank God, our story doesn't end there. We were on our way to defeat until we uncovered the baggage we brought in and developed a strategy to overcome it. It doesn't matter where you start, you get to decide where you are going. Mentoring, counseling, and marriage enrichment opportunities, such as classes, retreats, and conferences, helped us win against the baggage we brought into our marriage both consciously and unconsciously. We read every book about marriage we could get our hands on. We started attending marriage conferences and opening our relationship up to others who had successful relationships. We gained wisdom on how to make marriage work.

In marriage, there are challenges that can seem daunting, requiring a team to conquer. These challenges may include addictions to things such as pornography, substances, or sex, as well as various forms of abuse, including verbal, mental, physical, or emotional. Other obstacles such as volatile anger, low self-esteem, or mental illness can also be overwhelming. Whatever adversities you encounter from your past in your personal life or relationships, seek the necessary support and assistance to overcome them.

Don't allow the past to control you any longer and keep you from the successful relationship and marriage you deserve. Overcoming past baggage is a normal part of building a healthy relationship. As you will hear repeated many times in this book, most people drown because they will not raise their hand and let others know they need help. Please don't drown in a sea of lifeguards.

> *Overcoming past baggage is a normal part of building a healthy relationship.*

ENEMY OF YOUR SOUL

Another opponent couples face in marriage is the soul, or heart. The heart is like fertile ground where seeds can be planted and grown to produce fruit in our lives. Proverbs 4:23 says, "Above all else, guard your heart, for everything you do flows from it." The heart is a powerful force that drives your thoughts and actions; therefore, you must be mindful of what you allow to take root in your heart because everything you do flows from it. The type of seeds you allow to take root in your heart can produce good fruit or bad fruit. The seeds that produce good fruit are from God. God's seeds do not kill, steal, or destroy. On the contrary, God's seeds produce health, wholeness, and freedom to live a purposeful, abundant life. God's promise to people who meditate on His Word says, "He shall be like a tree planted by the rivers of water, that brings forth its fruit in its season, whose leaf also shall not wither; and whatever he does shall prosper" (Psalm 1:3 NKJV). Planting the seeds of God's Word and allowing them to take root in your heart is a critical part of living a prosperous, fruitful life.

God is not the only one who sows seeds in your relationships. Life brings with it both good and bad seeds. Some of life's bad seeds are sown in your heart through people, problems, and pain. You may not have control over the seeds that are planted, but you do have control over which seeds you allow to take root or germinate. Negative experiences such as hurt, pain, betrayal, rejection, abandonment, abuse, and neglect can plant seeds of negativity that yield bitter fruit in your life and relationships. As these seeds mature, they create sensitive areas in your heart that become land mines and triggers that are easily set off, producing dysfunction, disorder, and dissatisfaction in your relationship. This turmoil makes it challenging to find peace and fulfillment, leaving your relationships in a perpetual state of confusion and upheaval. These bad seeds are designed to stunt your growth, keep you stuck, and harden your heart. They are sown to keep you from living the plans and purposes God intends for your life.

In my own life, as I (Tondra) mentioned in chapter 1, my father sowed seeds of rejection and abandonment when he disowned and neglected my mother and me. These seeds left me with deep feelings of shame, worthlessness, and betrayal. As I allowed these seeds to germinate over time, before I knew it, I had built a fortress in my heart of bitterness and resentment to protect me from ever being hurt or betrayed by anyone again. I falsely believed if you cannot trust your own father to protect you, then no one can be trusted. Holding on to the pain and bitterness made me feel powerful and in control. Staying hurt served as a badge of honor, reminding me to stay away from people and people to stay away from me.

If my marriage was going to work, I had to let go of the pain and no longer listen to the accuser's voice inside my head lying to me about who I was, what I was worth, and who I could trust. Sometimes we use denial to avoid dealing with pain; if we don't acknowledge it, then it doesn't exist. I was in denial big time, afraid if I opened that door to the hurt and pain, then I would not be able to handle it or it would overwhelm me.

For example, I used humor to mask the hurt and shame. When someone asked me about my father and expressed any concern or compassion toward me, I would make a joke to quickly exit the awkward conversation. I would say, with a chuckle, "It's okay. You don't need to feel sorry for me. You can't miss what you never had." My response was my effort to dismiss and deflect from the gravity of the impact this situation would have had on any little girl. I thought healing was being strong, not allowing things to break you down or affect you emotionally. Boy, was I wrong! True healing is being strong enough to feel the pain and allow it to help you grow and become a better person.

The saying "Time heals all wounds" is not true. Wounds go through a process to heal. It's about what you do during that time that heals wounds. If you are simply allowing time to pass without working toward healing, your hurt and pain will be waiting on you until you get there. There is no way to get to the other side of pain except by going through it. Three critical steps are necessary to move through your pain. You need to drop it, mop it, and stop it.

STEP 1: DROP IT

The first step is to release the pain. Give yourself permission to feel what you feel. Keeping the pain bottled up inside does not take the pain away; it only delays the healing process. You will not be able to progress and move forward and heal until you acknowledge the pain and feel it. Once I allowed myself to acknowledge and experience the pain, then and only then could I begin to truly let it go. You must grieve if you want to release the pain and truly heal. I've heard some of my clients reveal a fear of opening the pain to let it out. They were afraid that they would get stuck in the pain or that the pain would be too much for them to bear or handle. They expressed concern because life must keep going; there was no time to fall apart and no one to put them back together again. Pain may come gushing in like a waterfall but will gradually slow down to a trickle. If we bury it inside of us, then it's always with us, slipping out in subtle, unconscious ways. This is how our past becomes our present as well as our future if we don't deal with it once and for all.

STEP 2: MOP IT

After you have acknowledged and released the pain, you have to cleanse your heart. You would mop up after there was a spill in your house. You would not sit in a mess without cleaning your house. The heart is no different; you have to clean house. Releasing the pain leads you into finding freedom. Freedom gives you a clean start to rewrite the narrative surrounding your pain into a narrative of healing, overcoming, and growth. I found freedom from my pain through forgiveness. Holding on to pain only builds a monument called bitterness and resentment, which makes you stuck and holds you back from moving forward in your life and relationships.

Forgiveness, with God's help, became my weapon. Forgiveness is a process; it doesn't mean you condone what was done to you. It is a decision to give up the right for vengeance, retribution, or negative thoughts toward the person who hurt you.[1] It enables you to be free from anger, bitterness, and resentment. Forgiveness is more about your freedom and peace than the offender's. When you hold on to hurt and unforgiveness, not only do you punish the person who hurt you, but you also punish yourself. This process keeps you stuck in the pain and negatively attached to the person who caused the pain. The old saying goes, "Unforgiveness is like drinking poison and expecting the other person to die." Learning to forgive my father gave me the capacity to love my husband as well as others in my life.

STEP 3: STOP IT

The priority is for you to stop allowing the fear of getting hurt to control your life and relationships. Stop letting the hurt and pain define you; that only makes matters worse and prolongs the healing process that we all long for. It's time to stop living your life in survival mode and decide to create the safe space you have desired so your soul can rest. When you are afraid of being hurt, you build walls to protect yourself. These walls keep you isolated, cut off, and disconnected from love and relationships. A part of the healing process is finding the courage to open yourself up and take down the walls. Taking the walls down will make you feel vulnerable again, but you cannot have a genuine relationship without the risk of being hurt. You should be more afraid of staying where you are and risking the opportunity to experience being truly loved. The walls keep you from experiencing love because love requires vulnerability.

When you let people in, you give yourself the opportunity to learn and experience a secure, safe relationship. A critical part of healing relational wounds is experiencing healthy relationships. Because I had the courage to go through these steps of healing, I get to experience unconditional love and acceptance from a man who is loyal, trustworthy, and faithful to stand by my side through good and bad times. I also get to experience the healthy version of myself, a nurturing person who loves and cares for people. I get to live a new story of redemption, healing, and overcoming.

ENEMY OF YOUR MIND

Another internal opponent you need to overcome is your mind. The brain is the most powerful organ in the body. It's responsible for everything in the body, from the way you move to the way you think. Neuroscientists discovered that "neurons that fire together wire together."[2] This means repetitive thoughts become activated and reinforced, causing them to become your automated response or way of thinking and perceiving. Because your thoughts influence your emotions, behavior, and choices, what you think and how you think is critical to the life you live and the relationships you have.

In fact, trauma research discovered that a person's perception of an event can have just as much of an impact on them as the actual event itself.[3] What you think about and what you focus on is what you see and eventually what you become. The mind can be a powerful enemy because it's like a command center that controls everything about you. If something has your mind, then it has you.

> *Because your thoughts influence your emotions, behavior, and choices, what you think and how you think is critical to the life you live and the relationships you have.*

When people fall into depression, their thinking may become distorted because depression is a lens that filters out the positive things and allows only the negative things to come through. Seeing things in an extremely negative light adds to a sense of hopelessness. When a person views their marriage and spouse through a negative lens, it blocks out the positive things about their relationship and spouse, leaving them only with negative feelings. A negative filter allows you to see only what your spouse did wrong, and it blocks out what they did right.

The human tendency is to focus on the negative, mistakes, failures, and disappointments.[4] Psychological evidence reveals negative thoughts tend to get ingrained quicker and stay longer in our memory and minds than positive thoughts.[5] Psychologists claim that it takes five positive interactions to counteract every negative one.[6]

When a husband focuses on all the things his wife does wrong, over time, it can give him a negative view of his wife, leading to an overall negative view of their relationship. This leads to negative interactions, leaving both partners with feelings of hurt, bitterness, and resentment. Once their hearts become hardened toward each other, feelings of hatred and disgust take over. In working with couples, I (Tondra) have always been amazed at the level of venom that is spewed during couples counseling sessions between people who once loved each other and wanted to spend the rest of their lives together. Hardened hearts can block out any positive feelings by not allowing any access of compassion, empathy, or love for each other.

To overcome the enemy of your mind, you must first gain control over what you think. Second Corinthians 10:5 says, "We demolish arguments and every pretension that sets itself up against the knowledge of God, and we take captive every thought to make it obedient to Christ." To regain control over what you think, you must be protective of what you look at, listen to, and read about. Fill your mind with things that will lead you to where you want to go, who you want to be, and what kind of relationships you want to have. Philippians 4:8 says, "Finally, brothers and sisters, whatever is true, whatever is noble, whatever is right, whatever is pure, whatever is lovely, whatever is admirable—if anything is excellent or praiseworthy—think about such things."

There is a wide body of research on the power of rehearsing positive thoughts. This approach is one of the tenets of cognitive therapy. Thinking positively of your spouse and your relationship is a powerful buffer when you are going through challenging times in life and in your relationship.[7] When you consciously direct your attention to focus on positive thoughts, you activate the brain's reward system, releasing dopamine and serotonin, which are the "feel-good" neurotransmitters. Over time, this can rewire the brain to magnify positive thoughts and experiences, improving your overall view of your spouse and your relationship. Thinking positively about your spouse will allow you to appreciate and value them more, producing a stronger bond and more rewarding relationship.

> *Healthy people and healthy couples are constantly changing and growing.*

The next step to overcome the enemy of your mind is to change old, ingrained habits, behaviors, and patterns that are not helping you thrive in your life and relationships. Your habits determine your future because your life moves in the direction of your habits. Researchers have found that over 40 percent of what we do every day is not a result of decisions but a result of habits.[8] For example, some people may think you decide to brush your teeth, turn on the coffee maker, or fix your bed. However, these are behaviors that were ingrained over time and became unconscious habits.

There may be patterns, behaviors, and habits you learned that are not healthy or beneficial for building a healthy relationship and marriage, such as the way you communicate and resolve conflict. Romans 12:2 says, "Do not conform to the pattern of this world, but be transformed by the renewing of your mind. Then you will be able to test and approve what God's will is—his good, pleasing and perfect will." Renewing your mind means doing away with unhealthy thought patterns and replacing them with true, godly ones to help you fulfill the plans and purposes God has for you and your marriage.

Lasting change takes place in the mind. If you try to change your behavior only, chances are you will go back to the way you are used to. Thank God, we are not stuck in our old mindsets. The brain has neuroplasticity, which allows it to correct signaling, rewire itself, and restore connections to make change happen in our brains.[9] You are not stuck in habits and patterns that no longer serve you. You can learn new things and create new habits.

Have you heard the saying "You can't teach an old dog new tricks"? This is not a true statement. You *can* teach an old dog new tricks. When George and I were first married and he would try to teach me a new way of doing something, I would say, "Don't try and change me. You knew how I was when you married me." You are *supposed* to change and grow in life and marriage. If you are not growing, then you are stuck. If you are not ready to grow and change, then you are not ready for marriage.

Healthy people and healthy couples are constantly changing and growing. You should be different in your fifties than you were in your twenties. When we learn new things, we grow. Having a growth mindset is very necessary for building a strong, healthy marriage. A growth mindset enables you to learn new ways to listen, talk, connect, and love each other. A fixed mindset means being stuck in your ways and unwilling to change. A growth mindset is critical in overcoming the enemy of your mind. Facing and overcoming both external and internal opponents that threaten to undermine your relationship is a critical step for an effective marriage game plan. These opponents stand between you and your desire to win in your marriage. Dealing with your baggage helps create a culture of safety and trust.

Look at the following chart to see the difference between having a growth mindset and a fixed mindset. Which mindset represents you currently? What adjustments do you need to make to adopt a growth mindset?

CHARACTERISTICS OF A FIXED MINDSET VERSUS A GROWTH MINDSET

Fixed Mindset	Growth Mindset
Avoids challenges (stays in comfort zone)	Embraces challenges
Rejects feedback (takes offense)	Welcomes feedback
Believes mistakes define you	Believes mistakes are a part of learning
Believes effort is fruitless	Believes effort leads to mastery
Hides or ignores flaws	Strengthens and develops flaws[10]

Putting It into Practice

QUESTIONS

1. What impacted you most from this chapter, and why?

2. What baggage (hurts, pain, experiences, relationships) are you carrying as individuals and as a couple? How will you address the baggage that's burdening your relationship?

3. List a few specific enemies (past, soul, and mind) that you've brought into and allowed to stay in your relationship that are negatively impacting your marriage.

4. What's one new skill you would like to learn or a new habit you would like to develop to become a better spouse?

5. How will you make thinking positively about your spouse and relationship a consistent habit?

COUPLE'S ACTIVITY: BACKGROUND REFLECTION

No matter how long you have been married, exploring and processing how your past shows up in your present is an ongoing process. Layers of your baggage are revealed and shed over time as you heal.

INDIVIDUAL REFLECTION

1. What was the best thing about your childhood? What was the most difficult?

2. How would you describe your parents' relationship?

3. How would you describe your relationship with your mom? Your dad?

4. What did your parents do well? What could they have done differently?

5. What family patterns or themes have been passed from one generation to the next (such as addiction, poverty, divorce, hard work, trust in God, etc.)?

6. How did your family deal with difficult emotions (such as conflict, grief, etc.)?

7. Did you experience any type of abuse growing up (such as physical, emotional, sexual, mental, spiritual)? Explain.

8. What hardships has your family experienced (such as traumatic events, financial difficulties, etc.)?

9. In what ways are you similar and different from your dad? And your mom?

10. How would you describe the emotional environment of the home you grew up in?

COUPLES REFLECTION

Take turns sharing your insights from the Individual Reflection section, and ask each other the following questions.

1. How did your experiences discussed in the previous section make you feel in the past?

2. How do they make you feel now?

3. How has your past shaped your view of yourself physically, mentally, emotionally, relationally, and spiritually?

4. What have you learned from these experiences?

5. What issues remain unresolved from your past or with your parents that you are aware of?

6. What action steps do we need to take based on the insights we have gained?

PRAYER POINTS TO CONSIDER

ACTION ITEMS
(What steps, actions, or decisions do you need to make or take?)

TIME-OUT
For further insights and practical tips from this chapter, take a time-out and view our short bonus video, "Time-Out: Facing and Overcoming Your Opponents," using this link or QR code:

https://davidccook.org/access

Access code: GamePlan

Chapter 6

TRUSTING YOUR TEAMMATE

Good teams become great ones when the members trust each other enough to surrender the "me" for the "we."

Phil Jackson

Trust is the foundation of every successful team. When the coach "loses the locker room," he has lost the players' confidence and trust in his ability to lead the team and make good decisions. When trust is lost, the team falls apart. The players stop believing in the team and stop looking out for its best interests. They are no longer willing to give their all or push themselves beyond their limits to see the team win. They feel the need to take care of and look out for themselves and protect their own interests. Lack of trust leads to individualism, which works against teamwork. When trust is lost, it can lead to a mentality of every man for himself.

In marriage, a lack of trust can be equally damaging. Losing trust in our spouse and relationship creates that same isolation and individualism that sports players experience when they stop trusting their teammates. Trust is a felt sense of safety and a belief that the other person has your best interests at heart. It's about putting yourself in a position to be hurt but believing that person will not hurt you.

Even though everyone is born with the ability to trust, life experiences can shape whether we see trust as positive and safe or negative and unsafe. Bad experiences can cause you to doubt your spouse's intentions and damage your ability to trust. I (Tondra) had trust issues from the beginning of our relationship. These issues were caused not by George but by other men in my life who had made trust a scary and unsafe place.

Whether trust has been lost before or during your relationship, it's critical to rebuild and continue to build trust in every season. Trust is hard to gain, easy to lose, and even harder to rebuild. Therefore, if you have someone's trust, know you have a valuable gift and do everything you can to keep it. Trust is not a conscious decision a person makes; it is what's earned through consistent trust-building behaviors over time. These consistent behaviors allow the brain to be rewired to trust again.

When I am doing marriage coaching with couples who have experienced a breach in trust, the person who has broken their spouse's trust often wants their spouse to move on quickly and just trust them. Expressing how sorry you are and saying you never meant to hurt your spouse are not enough to rebuild trust. Even promising never to betray them again is not enough. However, those actions are a start. You cannot force a person to trust you; trust is something you must earn through consistency and patience. When there has been a breach of trust, restoration requires repeated experiences of the promised new behavior.

For instance, if a wife continues to promise to make time to have sex with her husband, then consistently does not make time and follow through on her promise, the husband can lose trust that his wife really cares about him or the relationship. The husband may feel insecure as to whether his wife loves him or is attracted to him. Over time, the repeated letdown and disappointment erode trust as the husband starts to believe his wife does not have his best interests at heart.

When a car breaks down continuously and must be towed and repaired repeatedly, over time, the owner will eventually lose confidence and trust in the car to meet their transportation needs. Repeatedly being disappointed or let down by your spouse will eventually lead to a lack of trust. To rebuild trust, it is critical to give your spouse repeated experiences of new trust-building behaviors.

To betray someone's trust is to intentionally act disloyally toward a person to whom you owe allegiance or obligation. Betrayal occurs in various forms, including committing infidelity (sexual or emotional), being deceitful or secretive, breaking promises or agreements, neglecting your spouse's needs, prioritizing personal desires over the relationship, consistently disappointing your spouse, or practicing any other behavior that disregards your spouse's well-being.

Differing perceptions of betrayal exist among spouses, as betrayal is subjective. What constitutes a breach of trust varies from one individual to another, and only your spouse can articulate what actions make them feel vulnerable or insecure. What undermines trust in one relationship may not have the same impact in another. It's crucial to note that this discussion doesn't pertain to codependent relationships, which are discussed in chapter 3 as an unhealthy dynamic.

> *Trust is hard to gain, easy to lose, and even harder to rebuild.*

The advent of social media and technology has introduced additional avenues for eroding trust within marriages. As digital connections become more prevalent, there's a false sense of security that emboldens people to test boundaries. Actions such as not posting pictures of your spouse, neglecting to disclose your relationship status, or portraying oneself as single on social media can trigger feelings of hurt and mistrust. Social media also presents opportunities to reconnect with past crushes and ex-partners, opening the door to seemingly innocent interactions that can quickly escalate into inappropriate behavior, jeopardizing the safety and trust within the relationship.

Trust creates safety in your relationship, allowing for a deeper, more intimate connection. If your spouse does not feel safe in the relationship, it will be difficult for them to be open and vulnerable. Trust is the foundation of a healthy relationship. If you are struggling with trust, there is hope. You *can* build trust. It will take both of you working to establish and maintain a trusting relationship.

If your goal as a couple is to build or restore trust, the person who has been hurt by their spouse's disloyalty needs to allow their spouse the opportunity to earn their trust and acknowledge and affirm their spouse's efforts to win their trust back. Work to reassure your spouse that their efforts to restore trust are paying off by acknowledging and appreciating when they take steps to change their behaviors to make you feel safe. Also, don't continually throw their betrayal in their face. I had a client whose goal was to never let her husband forget how he had hurt her so he would never do it again. The problem with repeatedly rehearsing hurt and pain is that it keeps you stuck in the hurt and pain. It limits your ability as a couple to heal and restore trust.

If you are the person who has lost the trust of your spouse, then you need to demonstrate through bold, concrete actions that you are committed to making your spouse feel safe. This includes changing the behaviors that led to the mistrust, as well as responding to your spouse's vulnerabilities and concerns with trust-enhancing behaviors. These behaviors may include deleting your social media account, allowing your spouse to have the passwords to your phone and computer, or calling to check in with your spouse during the day. The goal in restoring trust is to make your spouse feel safe, secure, and confident that you are taking steps to protect them and the relationship.

For example, George and I attended a friend's outdoor birthday party. There were tons of people there. We were mingling separately as we are both outgoing people. After some time, George called me over and shared with me he felt uncomfortable watching me talking with a male friend who was going through a divorce at the time. George said it appeared from where he was standing that we were in a very close, intimate conversation for a very long time. My response was, "If that made you feel uncomfortable, I apologize, and you will never have to worry about feeling that way again." George said my response immediately disarmed him because he knew I would take the necessary actions to not put him in that position again. He knew I would protect him.

My response was a trust-building response. Non-trust-building responses would sound like: "I was not doing anything wrong." "You are overreacting." "Stop being jealous and insecure." "You don't trust me." Building trust requires deliberate actions and decisions that protect your spouse and your relationship.

Here are some practical ways to build and maintain trust in your relationship.

MAKE GOOD FINANCIAL DECISIONS

How you manage money and make financial decisions can undermine trust. Money often represents power and control in a relationship. How you handle money can make your spouse feel manipulated, deceived, or controlled. Conflict surrounding money is one of the top issues that can lead to divorce.[1]

Sometimes couples think if they had more money, then they wouldn't have problems, but conflict surrounding finances affects couples from all socioeconomic levels. Some would say the more money you have, the more problems you have.

Conflicts over money stem from having different money styles and approaches. A "saver" may be married to a "spender." A saver is someone who wants to hold on to their money. They like to see their savings increase, not decrease. A spender is someone who may think, *I make money to spend it enjoying life and the things I want*. George is the spender, and I am the saver. I desire to save money because it makes me feel secure when I can see we have money in the bank. George, on the other hand, desires to spend money to see he is providing a good life for his family by doing nice things for me and the kids.

Finances are deeply personal and intimate, often intertwined with fears and ingrained beliefs that influence financial decisions. Research indicates that individuals inherit attitudes, values, and beliefs about money from their family upbringing.[2] When couples have differing approaches to money management, it can erode trust in each other's financial capabilities and decision-making. This disparity may lead to suspicions that one's spouse doesn't have their best interests at heart, prompting secretive behaviors such as maintaining hidden accounts or making undisclosed purchases. It's essential for couples to openly communicate and work together to navigate financial challenges and build trust in their relationship.

When working with premarital couples, I found that some couples had not discussed finances at all, despite their weddings being around the corner. It's not untypical for engaged couples not to have discussed finances in depth. Some are resistant to show each other their financial portfolio because they may feel that it's none of their partner's business. They believe that whatever they acquired before marriage belongs solely to them and is not relevant to their future marriage. There are couples who call off their weddings because their partner will not sign a prenuptial agreement. Discussing and agreeing on finances early on makes a difference.

Unfortunately, many couples don't realize the significance financial values, beliefs, and attitudes have when it comes to building trust in their marriage. It is extremely important to discuss finances and ensure you understand each other's financial backgrounds and views as well as develop a game plan as you move forward. Here are some practical things you can do to make good financial decisions as a couple, which will build trust in your marriage.

KEEP AN OPEN, ONGOING DIALOGUE ABOUT YOUR FINANCES

Regular communication helps you get on the same page and stay on the same page about your finances. This will prevent surprises and unexpected discoveries, which lead to mistrust. Set a regular check-in time each month to sit down and pay bills or discuss your expenses and savings plan. Oftentimes people don't see eye to eye when it comes to finances, so you both must be willing to compromise. Each of you must be open to sacrificing something to find agreement. The more a couple agrees on their financial approach, the more they will feel safe and establish trust.

DEVELOP AN AGREED-UPON SPENDING PLAN

Having a game plan for your finances is a critical part of having a successful overall marriage game plan. Doing finances haphazardly will prevent you from accomplishing the things in life that are important to you. To be financially responsible means you know how much money you have, how much money you are spending, and how much money you are saving. A plan builds trust and confidence when making financial decisions.

As a couple, decide what goals you want to save for and what you want to spend your money on. It is also helpful to decide on a monthly personal spending limit. This is the amount each of you can spend without having to check in with each other. You will need to discuss and agree on any spending above this allowance amount.

For example, you set a limit of five hundred dollars. Each of you can spend under that amount freely, but anything above five hundred dollars you will decide on together. This allows each of you to feel a level of freedom and independence to not have to get permission for everything you buy. It keeps you both accountable to the financial goals you have set. Lastly, it's not enough to have a plan; both spouses must honor and be faithful to the plan.

BOTH SPOUSES TAKE AN ACTIVE ROLE

When you're married, your financial choices no longer affect solely yourself; they also impact your spouse and children. Collaborating as a team regarding finances is crucial. Both partners share responsibility for family finances as they significantly influence quality of life. Consequently, managing all the stress and pressure alone can become problematic over time.

I (Tondra) remember counseling a couple where the husband was the breadwinner and the wife was a stay-at-home mom. The family fell into financial trouble, and the wife did not want their lifestyle to change. She refused to work even part-time because her dream was to be a stay-at-home mom. Nor did she want to downsize the home. The husband was under extreme stress and pressure. It's not fair for the family finances to rest on one person alone while the other person completely checks out of any financial responsibility. When both spouses take an active role, it builds trust because you know you have each other's back and neither one of you is in this alone.

When both spouses take an active role in the family finances, it also provides checks and balances. Maybe one person pays the bills, and the other person schedules the monthly meetings to discuss the financial outlook. You need a joint strategy where both parties know about the family's financial goals, agree to them, and take responsibility to reach them.

When it comes to financial decision-making, we're not financial experts by any means. However, we've shared some of the valuable best practices we've gleaned on our journey with marriage and money. Prioritizing financial matters is crucial due to their profound impact on trust within your marriage. Therefore, don't hesitate to seek professional financial guidance through financial planners, workshops, and classes.

GET RID OF THE PLAN-B MENTALITY

When you have a plan-B mentality, it's hard to commit yourself to a plan A wholeheartedly. Holding on to plan B does not foster an environment of trust and safety. When you have a plan B, you work at something differently than you do when you have no other option. In the back of your mind, you know you have a backup just waiting to be executed. A plan-B mentality leads you to become a spectator in your relationship, sitting back and constantly analyzing and deciding whether this is the plan you want. For instance, if a wife gives her wedding ring back to her husband every time he doesn't do something how and when she wants it, she is unconsciously asking her husband to prove himself to be a better option than her plan B, which could be another man, a separate bank account, or another place to live.

You cannot have a healthy marriage with one foot in and one foot out. Not being all in creates a roller coaster of anxiety and uncertainty in the relationship, causing each person to go into self-preservation mode. Where there is a lack of stability and consistency, there is a lack of trust. You are either all in or all out. Removing other options allows you to give 100 percent of yourself to making your marriage work.

> *You cannot have a healthy marriage with one foot in and one foot out.*

When you wholeheartedly commit to your spouse and your relationship, you foster a secure environment where vulnerability and intimacy can flourish. This level of commitment transitions you from a mere spectator in your marriage to an active participant. Consider NFL stadiums across the country, filled with spectators passively watching twenty-two men compete on the field, giving their all to win the game. While spectators remain in a state of observation, participants take decisive action. In marriage, actively engaging means you're contributing to the success of your marriage. No longer content to sit back and watch, you're fully invested in making your marriage thrive.

Remember, what you invest in your marriage directly influences what you gain. Sustaining a fulfilling marriage requires effort. When your spouse witnesses your dedication and effort, it fosters trust and security because it shows them that they're not facing challenges alone. The key to a successful marriage lies in both spouses diligently working together, compromising, and finding solutions collaboratively.

A great teammate never leaves a man or woman behind. You win together, or you fail together. Whatever the outcome, you go through it together. Successful sports teams encourage each other whether they win or lose because they know they are fighting together for a common goal and they don't have to fight alone. They celebrate the hard work each person sacrificed for the good of the team and for each other. Teams who focus only on outcomes are not successful in the long game because over time they fall apart. Winning teams are all in. The players help their team win by focusing on putting their work in and bringing their best selves to the game because they know the team is counting on them.

A plan-B mentality is focused on outcomes, and when you are focused on outcomes, your focus is not on helping your team with everything you can. When you're focused on outcomes, as soon as things don't go your way, you are ready to walk away and give up. Your spouse cannot depend on you to ride through the ups and downs of life together. When your spouse can't count on you, they can't trust you.

I (Tondra) was coaching a couple where the husband wanted his wife to be more intentional about making him a priority in their relationship. The husband was waiting for his wife to change, and after a few days he would point out every time and every way she did not make him a priority. He did this just to prove the marriage was not going to work. This husband felt his wife was the only one who needed to change, and if she didn't make the necessary changes, then it was over. The husband was operating as a spectator in his marriage. He saw the problem as a "you" problem, not a "we" problem. As a participator, he would have seen himself as part of the solution. The wife said it was hard to make him feel like a priority when his attitude and the tension she felt around him made her want to avoid him and withhold doing nice things for him. Both people are a part of the solution in marriage.

Being *all in* means the team cannot win without every member doing their part. An elite athlete's work ethic, or how hard an athlete works, separates them from a talented athlete, just as a couple's work ethic can determine whether their marriage thrives or simply survives. Here are some practical things you can do to be all in and build trust in your marriage, making it an elite marriage:

> **1. Don't take shortcuts.** A good work ethic involves grit, drive, and determination. Elite athletes don't take shortcuts, because they know the benefits of working hard. They understand that "no pain equals no gain." They know if you are going to be elite, it's going to cost you something. The greatest

rewards cost you time and effort and sacrifice. You don't become great overnight. As couples, you have to invest in your marriage and work hard at it, strengthening your marriage by attending retreats, going on date nights, and building communication skills. There are no shortcuts in building an elite marriage.

2. **Find a way to win.** Elite athletes are dedicated to "the game" above all else. They demonstrate dedication through unwavering commitment, making sacrifices to improve, achieve, and succeed. Elite marriages possess the same level of commitment and sacrifice. They don't give up when things get hard and challenging. They do the opposite: they press in more to push through any obstacles threatening their efforts in order to succeed.

3. **Welcome coaching.** Elite athletes don't get to the professional level without allowing coaches to speak into their lives. They understand that to make it to an elite level, they need help. Coaching is essential to reach their highest potential. The same is true for couples wanting to be successful in marriage. Couples who are most successful realize the value of coaching. They seek out resources, mentors, and professionals to help them be successful.

COMMIT TO COVENANT COMMUNICATION

When you commit to covenant communication, you build trust in your relationship. Covenant communication is communication that aligns and reinforces the vows you made on your wedding day, especially if those vows were biblical vows. On that day, you made a covenant, a sacred promise, with your spouse before God and family. Covenant communication is communicating in a way that upholds and reinforces your covenant and shows honor and respect for your spouse and the value they bring to you and your life.

On your wedding day you received and committed yourselves to each other. Receiving your spouse is not a one-time thing; it is a continual, daily choice to honor and respect. This commitment is expressed through the way you communicate with your spouse. The Bible says, "The tongue has the power of life and death, and those who love it will eat its fruit" (Prov. 18:21). Your words have the ability to give life or to destroy your relationship. You can cause lasting emotional damage to your spouse and destroy their trust by belittling them, making them feel less than, or viewing them with condescension and contempt rather than love and respect. When a person doesn't feel valued in the relationship, it's very hard to trust that the other person has their best interests at heart.

Dr. John Gottman studied and analyzed communication patterns in thousands of couples for more than forty years. His research found that the way a couple fights predicts whether they will divorce.[3] The way you communicate with your spouse has a significant impact on the quality and longevity of your relationship. In the same way covenant communication can build trust, destructive communication can destroy it.

Covenant communication doesn't happen by chance. It requires deliberate effort to engage in communication that fosters healthy interactions, upholds your vows, builds trust, and strengthens the bond between you and your spouse. If you've ever played darts, you understand the goal is to hit the bull's-eye, which is impossible without focus. Similarly, achieving the mark of covenant communication demands focused attention. Here are some key focal points to help you hit the bull's-eye.

> *Your words have the ability to give life or to destroy your relationship.*

FOCUS ON THE FACTS, NOT THE FEELINGS

We can get offtrack if we allow our feelings to control us. You cannot allow your feelings to master you. There is a difference between being in control and being controlled. In football there is a saying, "Control what you can control." It means you cannot control everything that is going on in the game and you cannot control other people but you can control yourself, your actions, and your emotions. If you allow your feelings to be in charge, they can deceive you because feelings don't tell the truth about what's going on. The Bible says, "The heart is deceitful above all things, and desperately wicked; who can know it?" (Jer. 17:9 NKJV). But the facts are the facts; they reveal the truth about what's going on.

Feelings have a role, but they are not the whole story. Feelings can signal there is something a couple needs to explore further, much like an indicator light in a car tells you there is a problem that you need to check out. You must find out what the signal is trying to tell you to fully resolve the issue. As couples, you must explore what your feelings are trying to tell you individually and as a couple. To explore these emotional triggers, you must gather the facts by asking yourself questions like these:

- Who am I upset with?
- Why is this so triggering to me?
- What expectations or needs were not met?
- Where have I been let down?
- How have I been disappointed?

Once you gather the facts, they will lead you to the truth. For example, I was struggling to adjust as a new mom, and George, Mr. Fix-It-and-Improve-It Man, suggested it would be a good idea to get some advice from a friend who had been a mother longer. This comment was emotionally triggering to me. George could not understand what he had done wrong, as he was only trying to be helpful. Exploring my feelings led me to recognize the fact that George's suggestion tapped into my fears and beliefs that I was not good enough because of my upbringing. Once I understood the facts, they led me to the truth. George was not saying I was not good enough as a mom. The opposite was in fact true. He loves me, married me, and chose me to be the mother of his kids. George was trying to support me and not see me struggle as a new mom. This process also enabled us to have a productive conversation, and he reinforced the truth that I was indeed good enough.

The next time you are triggered, reflect before you react. First, slow things down by taking some deep breaths, counting backward from ten, and calming yourself down. Then, ask yourself some questions like, *What am I feeling, and why am I feeling it?* Next, don't indict your spouse; instead ask your spouse clarifying questions such as, "When you said _____, what did you mean?" Or "Am I hearing you say _____?" Once you understand your feelings and gather the facts, then you can communicate more effectively with your spouse. This requires patience and self-control, and it may take some time and practice to develop these skills, but with God's help and your determination, you can do it. Don't give up. The Bible says, "In the multitude of words sin is not lacking, but he who restrains his lips is wise" (Prov. 10:19 NKJV).

FOCUS ON CLEAR, DIRECT COMMUNICATION

Covenant communication is clear and direct and does not involve mind reading or making assumptions. You must verbalize expectations in order to give your spouse an opportunity to meet those expectations. I (Tondra) have spoken to many wives who believe if their husbands truly knew them, they would know their expectations. I quickly tell those ladies, "They don't know." Your spouse really doesn't know if you don't tell them. Expectations must be clearly stated, discussed, and agreed upon.

Communication is a two-way street. It involves talking and listening. The speaker must speak to be understood. Determine what you want to say and how you want to say it. Make sure your body language, tone, and words are congruent. For example, when a wife verbally says "I'm fine; nothing is wrong" but her body language says something totally different, she throws mixed signals.

Lastly, you must determine when you want to have the conversation. Timing is key when you want to communicate something important. Timing is important because it allows you to be heard and understood. When your spouse is tired, hungry, or distracted, they are not going to be fully focused on what you are saying. In fact, they could be impatient and irritable, which is most likely going to lead to an argument. Also, if you have something you want your spouse to hear and understand, it is best not to do it when you are feeling extremely upset or angry. Chances are it will be difficult for you to communicate without making your spouse feel attacked and defensive.

George and I like to break our communication up into zones. We have a work zone and a free zone. Work zones are times to work on things you need to address as a couple, such as working on your relationship or handling family business. Reserving these types of conversations for the work zone prevents us from bringing up tough conversations at the wrong time.

Free zones are to enjoy personal time and each other without fear of being blindsided by conversations that may spark tension. Free zones can include video games, sports or TV shows, bedtime, date night, or dinnertime.

These zones help us compartmentalize our conversations, keeping us on the same page. For example, if George is getting into bed thinking he's going to sleep and I bring up something that annoyed me that day, we're not going to have a productive conversation. Similarly, a couple will not have a good date night if the husband brings up an old argument that was never resolved. Implementing these zones also serves as a safeguard against overlooking or disregarding important aspects of your relationship that require attention.

The listener's role in covenant communication is to listen to understand. To seek understanding, you cannot focus on your point of view or your objection to what's being shared. The Bible says, "Fools find no pleasure in understanding but delight in airing their own opinions" (Prov. 18:2). The listener's job is to ask questions and remain curious to understand their spouse's perspective and point of view. The listener needs to take notes of the main points. The listener communicates understanding when they can internalize and summarize what they heard and understood. To be a good listener takes empathy. Empathy is putting yourself in the other's shoes to become familiar with what's going on with them internally. Proverbs 18 also says, "To answer before listening—that is folly and shame" (v. 13).

FOCUS ON THE BIG PICTURE

Holding on to things will work against covenant communication. When you dwell on or become hyper-focused on mistakes or failures, then you become stuck and forward progress is halted. You cannot achieve victory and success when you can't move forward. Successful teams know how to keep the big picture in mind. The NFL has shown how important it is to have a short-term memory.

When a team loses a game, there is a time to mourn, to look at what mistakes they made or what they missed. But they must quickly turn the page and begin preparing for and focusing on the next game. During a game when a play doesn't work right, they must quickly shake it off and move on. When a team or an athlete holds on too long to a mistake, it can affect the next game or the next play on the field and jeopardize the entire game or the entire season.

As couples, when you keep harping on tough moments or tough seasons of your marriage, you can become stuck, continually throwing mistakes and failures in your spouse's face. When this happens, both spouses can grow bitter and resentful, which in turn leads to negative, hurtful language and communication that destroys trust in your relationship.

MAINTAIN INTIMACY INTEGRITY

Another area where trust can be quickly lost is in the area of sexual intimacy. When a person doesn't feel valued and appreciated, it's tough for them to feel safe and trusting in the relationship. One of the first places where lack of trust appears is the bedroom. Sex is a very intimate, vulnerable situation; it requires trust for a person to expose themselves to that level of depth. If you can't take care of your spouse emotionally, then it will be hard for them to trust that you can take care of them physically.

Intimacy integrity is built well before you get to the bedroom. George had a mentor who taught him, "If you want the house hot at night, then you have to light the fire in the morning." As a couple, you maintain intimacy integrity when you prioritize your spouse and do not take them for granted. Sometimes when you are married, you get so caught up in the routines of who takes out the trash or who picks up the kids from school, you can forget to be grateful for and appreciative of your spouse.

Selfishness destroys intimacy.

You maintain intimacy integrity when you focus on your spouse and not on yourself. Selfishness destroys intimacy. Intimacy requires being selfless, making sacrifices, and making your relationship and spouse a priority. Sometimes people place a high value on their career or children, prioritizing them over the marriage relationship. This is backward thinking. It is the marriage relationship that is the foundation of the life you are building.

The marriage relationship is like the roots of a tree, which keep the tree grounded, alive, and thriving. Everything you do for the family flows from the marital roots; therefore, making sure the roots are nourished and taken care of is critical. When your marriage is thriving, it helps you produce at work and your children feel safe and secure. What is the point of losing your family because of the career you wanted so you could support and provide a good life for your family? Also, children are to be supported by the safety of the marriage covenant. The greatest gift you can give your children is a healthy marriage that reflects God's character and nature.

George received a note from our daughter, Camryn, as she was going off to college a few years ago. She wrote, "I am beyond blessed to live in a household so full of love and support. You and mom have created an environment for me to excel in. I am not only able to see what a couple still married after 26 years looks like, but I get to see what a couple still madly in love after 26 years looks like! I aspire to have a marriage like you and mom. One full of love, patience, communication and most importantly founded in God." You can only imagine what receiving this meant to George and me. This note is a beautiful example of the result of making your spouse and relationship a priority, aligning with God's intended plan for the family. When your priorities are out of order, things can fall apart.

You maintain intimacy integrity when you value your teammate. In marriage, you are a team, and each teammate has value; one person is not more important than the other. The ESPN/Netflix documentary series *The Last Dance* is about the Chicago Bulls basketball team and their star player, Michael Jordan. He was the big personality on the team, and everything revolved around him. Scottie Pippen and the rest of the Chicago Bulls team felt overshadowed by Michael Jordan's fame and hype. Scottie Pippen didn't feel like his career, development, and success could reach its full potential in Michael Jordan's shadow. George and I like to say there are no Michael Jordans and no Scottie Pippens in marriage. Each person and their contribution matters. No one person can be great alone in marriage.

You must be intentional in making sure your spouse feels significant and valued. You value your spouse when you are intentional about investing quality time in your relationship. Time equals love. Actions speak louder than words. Here are a few practical ways to build trust through intimacy integrity:

Listen to your spouse. Listen with your ears, not your mouth. Listening helps your spouse feel understood.

Make eye contact. Looking your spouse in the eyes makes them feel seen. Eye contact always deepens connection by helping you mirror what your spouse is feeling.

Validate their emotions. When you validate their emotions, your spouse feels important and cared for.

Be easily reachable. When your spouse can reach you when you are not together, they feel prioritized. It shows them that no matter what's going on or where you are, they can reach you if they need you.

Defend them to others. When you defend your spouse, they feel protected and not alone. Defending them shows your allegiance to them and the relationship. In times where your spouse is wrong, you can still defend their honor and address in private what they did wrong. For example, in public, you might say, "That's my wife [or husband] you are speaking to [or talking about]. I can't allow you to do that."

Support their goals. When what's important to them is important to you, your spouse feels like you believe in them. You can support your spouse by attending events with them or learning about the thing they are interested in. For example, when you come across an article about their interest or hear about a class on it, you pass on the information to them.

Have shared experiences. Doing things together as a couple, especially when you take risks together, builds friendship in your marriage. Getting outside of your comfort zone allows you to share in a challenge or struggle, which can bond you closer together.

Give physical affection. The skin is the body's biggest organ. It is alive and needs to be nurtured. When you hold hands, cuddle, hug, and kiss each other, oxytocin is released. Oxytocin is a bonding hormone. The more you touch, the more you bond.

Give verbal appreciation. When you give verbal appreciation, you make your spouse feel loved and show they are not taken for granted. Sometimes I hear spouses say, "My spouse should know how I feel about them because I show them." Showing them is great! However, words are also important. The Bible says, "Gracious words are a honeycomb, sweet to the soul and healing to the bones" (Prov. 16:24). Your words have power to heal and refresh your spouse.

Ask deep questions. When you ask deep questions, you get to know your spouse more. You never outgrow getting to know your spouse. You and your spouse are continuously evolving as life shapes you; therefore, what you know about your spouse in one season is not the same as what you need to know about them in another season.

Pursue reciprocity. When you have reciprocity in your relationship, you give as well as receive. In unbalanced relationships, one person does the taking and the other person does all the giving. Reciprocity is needed for a balanced relationship. Each spouse must give and receive.

Take responsibility. Taking responsibility for your actions builds respect and trust with your spouse. When you've done something wrong, own it and ask for forgiveness.

Follow through. Let your word be your word. If you say you are going to do something, work hard to follow through. If you can't follow through, then follow up and let your spouse know if adjustments or changes need to be made. Following up lets your spouse know that you have not forgotten what you said and that it's important to you to follow through.

Grow together spiritually. When you grow together spiritually, you both work to have a godly life and relationship.

Trust is the foundation of every winning team. Being intentional about building trust by making financial decisions together, upholding your commitment to each other, fostering covenant communication, and maintaining intimacy can establish and strengthen trust in every season of marriage. Trust-building behaviors create many positive moments to celebrate and build your friendship with your spouse.

Putting It into Practice

QUESTIONS

1. What impacted you most from this chapter, and why?

2. What are two trust-building behaviors your spouse does that make you feel secure in your relationship?

3. List two things you can do to increase your communication about finances.

4. Who could play the role of a relationship coach in your marriage?

5. What listening and speaking skills do you need to develop to foster covenant communication?

6. Describe one change you can make this week to demonstrate that when it comes to your relationship, you are all in.

7. What can each of you do to make romance and intimacy a priority in your marriage?

8. Each of you take a moment to reminisce about a time when you two had the best sex. Share your answer and three things that made the moment so special.

COUPLE'S ACTIVITY: DATE NIGHT

Each of you create a list of six date ideas that you both would love to experience together. Exchange these lists and take turns planning one idea from your spouse's list each month. One month the husband plans a date from his wife's list, and the next month the wife plans a date from her husband's list. By doing so, each of you will plan six dates for the year, resulting in twelve memorable outings.

ZONES ACTIVITY

As a couple, agree on work zones, times during the week to work on things you need to address as a couple—for example, your relationship or family business. This will keep you from bringing up tough conversations at the wrong time.

Agree on times during the week that are free to enjoy personal time and each other without fear of being blindsided by conversations that may spark tension (free zones). These times may include playing video games, watching sports or TV, at bedtime, date night, or dinnertime.

COVENANT COMMUNICATION ACTIVITY

Covenant communication is a powerful way to build trust in your relationship by communicating honor and respect. This way of communicating helps protect your relationship from destructive and damaging communication patterns that eventually lead to divorce. The goal of this activity is to enable you to cultivate healthy interactions that not only uphold your vows but also fortify the connection between you and your spouse.

Directions: Engage in the conversation points below by taking turns as the speaker and listener. Adhere to the speaker and listener guidelines provided for each role.

CONVERSATION POINTS

- What is most satisfying about our relationship currently, and why?
- How can I be a better spouse for you during this season?
- What are your deepest fears about our future together?

SPEAKER GUIDELINES

- **What do you want to say?** Express your needs and desires. Articulate clearly what you want your spouse to know. Journaling your thoughts first may be helpful.
- **How do you want to say it?** Make sure your body language, tone, and words are congruent, so you don't send mixed messages.
- **Speak the truth with love.** Be authentic and vulnerable; however, don't use negatively charged words, attacking speech, or accusations.
- **Describe yourself and your own feelings.** Express your own emotions and experiences rather than your perspective of what your spouse has done or failed to do. Beginning sentences with "I" instead of "you" will be helpful.

LISTENER GUIDELINES

- **Listen to understand.** Be present (not thinking of responses, rebuttals, disagreement, or opinions).
- **Manage your emotions.** Don't allow your personal feelings about what's being said to take over and prevent you from listening.
- **Be curious.** Ask clarifying questions to gain more understanding, such as:
  - Would you like advice, or would you like me to just listen?
  - Help me understand why this is so important to you.
  - What I'm hearing you say is _____. Am I missing anything?
  - What do you want me to know most about what you shared?
  - Can you give me more context or background?
- **Summarize what you heard.** Take notes if you need to. What are their needs, how are they feeling, and why is this important to them?

QUESTIONS: DISCUSS YOUR RESPONSES WITH YOUR SPOUSE

1. What is one thing you learned about your spouse through this activity?

2. How will you apply what you learned about covenant communication?

PRAYER POINTS TO CONSIDER

ACTION ITEMS
(What steps, actions, or decisions do you need to make or take?)

TIME-OUT

For further insights and practical tips from this chapter, take a time-out and view our short bonus video, "Time-Out: Trusting Your Teammate," using this link or QR code:

https://davidccook.org/access

Access code: GamePlan

Chapter 7

VICTORY MONDAYS

The best thing about marriage is friendship.
Friedrich Nietzsche

There are not many things greater on any team than the feeling of winning together. Sports teams compete against each other in hopes of being declared the winner when the clock hits zero and the final buzzer sounds. After a victory, locker rooms are filled with big smiles, cheering, and competitive banter about who dominated on the field like true warriors. But a win never ends with just a feeling of accomplishment. It includes other perks.

The icing on any winner's cake is when the coach declares, "Victory Monday!" Victory Monday (or whatever day comes after a competitive win) is about celebrating the big accomplishment of winning together. It's about earning a day off from competition and practice to rest in knowing what the team's effort and hard work accomplished.

In those moments, athletes and coaches will not focus on what needs to be improved or where the game could have been played better. There will be other times for critical review. Instead, players and coaches focus on celebrating the big win together and honoring one another. It's exciting to see players not only congratulate their teammates but also express their need for what each teammate brought to the victory. In those moments you see a sense of true affirmation that everyone's talent, strength, and effort was needed and felt. There is a sense of acknowledging that the win was a team effort, not a solo one.

VICTORY MONDAYS IN MARRIAGE

The feeling of winning is essential in the marital bond and team. Spouses often feel a closer bond of love and affection when wins in the relationship are celebrated. When an overcritical and nitpicky atmosphere dominates a relationship, there is trouble in the water. In marriage, couples, like sports teams, want to win. Spouses want to know their collective contribution to the relationship is helping the marriage team and family win together.

We think couples could learn a lot from the sports concept of Victory Mondays. If couples would incorporate regular Victory Monday times within their relationship, they would experience more marital satisfaction and moments of joy and appreciation. A study published in the journal *Personal Relationships* found that higher levels of marital satisfaction and connection are achieved when gratitude and appreciation are prevalent in marriage.[1] Moments of celebration as a couple, no matter how big or small, make both spouses feel a greater sense of love and appreciation.

Celebrating wins together is essential, whether it's accomplishing a goal, raising kids, or creating an environment of togetherness where the family can give and receive love. But winning in your relationship is a lot different from winning on a field or court. Because there are no winners or losers based on gameplay in marriage, couples must have a sense of gauging whether they are winning in their marriage during every season. But how can we define winning in marriage? During our thirty years of marriage, we've found that a strong friendship bond correlates to a winning marriage.

FRIENDSHIP VERSUS THE FEELING OF BEING IN LOVE

Many people would say that love is the most important ingredient in a successful and winning marriage. However, the feeling of being in love can be fleeting based on the season and circumstances of our relationship. In fact, we have told countless premarital couples that it takes more than being in love to have a happy and satisfying relationship. When the feeling of being in love has faded or feels like a thing of the past, you need something more to keep the relationship alive.

Couples often feel as if they chose the wrong partner or are in the wrong relationship when the feeling of being in love dissipates over time. The hit single "After the Love Has Gone" by Earth, Wind & Fire expresses this sentiment:

> *After the love has gone*
> *What used to be right is wrong.*[2]

When couples find themselves experiencing these feelings of waning or lost love, there must be something that outlasts the feeling of being in love. We think this "something" is friendship. Building and cultivating friendship in marriage is foundational for marital satisfaction. Friendship keeps couples feeling connected and turning to each other long after the feeling of being in love comes and goes like waves on a shore. If a spouse goes through a season of not feeling in love and an endearing friendship has not been cultivated, it will not be long before marriage feels like a duty and obligation.

> *Building and cultivating friendship in marriage is foundational for marital satisfaction.*

When couples come to us with issues of marital dissatisfaction, the problems typically surround some recurring issue that they have become hypersensitive to and focused on. That's why we rarely start with addressing the problem when we start coaching a couple. We typically begin by asking the couple how they fell in love and decided to get married. This question inevitably takes their minds off the problem and leads them to remember key moments of love, passion, and bonding. Often they will recall long walks and talks and hours spent together laughing and just having fun. Immediately the problems somehow fade into the background as they remember the days of bonding and kindling their new love and friendship.

THE BREAKDOWN OF FRIENDSHIP IN A MARRIAGE

Many things can cause a good marriage to seem disappointing, as though defeat has set in. Constant negativity, acrimony, and a focus on all that is going wrong can bring any couple to question their love and devotion to each other. When couples find themselves in this space, they inevitably reach a point of marital dissatisfaction and feel disconnected and detached. Prolonged periods of not feeling connected and on the same team often lead to disengagement and withdrawal. This is why it is vitally important to shut down a culture of negativity and criticism in your relationship.

Let's face it: Some of us have become professionals at pointing out our spouses' wrongdoings and areas in which they can simply do better. We've become somewhat like the nightmare referees who throw penalty flags or blow whistles at so many small errors that the game is no fun to watch or play. For those in marriages who experience the referee spouse, like crowds chanting angrily at a ball game, we say, "Let them play, ref! Let them play!" Don't get me wrong: we all have areas where we need to improve, but none of us want to constantly hear where we've erred and messed up.

I (George) have at times been hypercritical and too vocal on ways Tondra could improve in our marriage and family. Most of those times I was not even aware of what I was doing as it was just in my nature to point things out. That is until one day Tondra turned to me and said, "What do I do right in this marriage?" She was conveying that my constant critical nature was demoralizing her and she needed to hear something positive instead. Couples need to be more self-aware and hit the pause button on overly focusing on the problems. A litany of problems creates a cloud over the relationship that makes it almost impossible to see the progress or the winning moments.

We advise couples to try a two-step approach to offsetting the natural habit of focusing on negative things or things that need to be worked on. This approach, although simple, can have a big impact on your marriage or relationship. The two-step approach involves acknowledging and celebrating. The approach of acknowledging and celebrating often requires building new habits, which, for some couples and individuals, might be a bit of a challenge. But in the end, those new ways of doing things can change the landscape in any marriage or relationship. When couples work hard at accentuating the positive aspects of their relationship over time, it becomes easier to not overly focus and dwell on the negative aspects.

These steps have their foundation in the popular 1944 song lyrics "Ac-Cent-Tchu-Ate the Positive":

> *You've got to*
> *Ac-cent-tchu-ate the positive,*
> *E-lim-mi-nate the negative,*
> *Latch on to the affirmative,*
> *Don't mess with Mister In-Between.*[3]

In these lyrics, we are challenged with not focusing solely on the negative but instead taking more time to accentuate and highlight positive things in the relationship. Learning to not major on negative things and times leaves more room to latch on to the positive aspects of the relationship. Mastering this has the potential to be a transformative game changer for couples.

ACKNOWLEDGE

In this step, we simply outwardly acknowledge growth or evolution in our spouse when we notice change or when they do something that we prefer, especially if we've been critical of whenever they've gotten it wrong in the past. When we positively acknowledge growth in our spouse, it is like rays of sun that penetrate dark skies on a cloudy day.

For instance, if your spouse is constantly late getting to places and it has been an issue that has challenged your relationship in the past, trust me, they know when they've disappointed you. Instead of solely pointing out when they arrive late, try acknowledging when they do arrive at a place on time. Most likely your spouse will respond more positively to your acknowledgment of the times when they get it right than your negative acknowledgment when they don't measure up.

When we verbally take note of our spouse's attempt to change for the better, they will start to see how much of a positive effect it has on you as their partner and the relationship overall. Accentuating and acknowledging the positive moments helps reinforce how positive change brings more harmony and satisfaction. Conversely, when we only point out when our spouse does not measure up or when they get something wrong, it brings an overall sense of a lack of harmony and dissatisfaction. Remember, one of the goals in your marriage is to win together, not tear each other down on the way.

> *One of the goals in your marriage is to win together, not tear each other down on the way.*

Avoid using this strategy of acknowledging as a way to give your spouse a backhanded compliment. When you see your spouse improve in an area, don't use sarcasm to bring up past times of struggle. Nothing kills a moment of trying to grow or get better in an area like sarcasm and ridicule. Avoid saying things like, "So I see you are finally on time after years of being late," or "Wow, you finally did not show up late." Things like this often cause our spouse not to try to change or meet us halfway.

Instead, you want to show them that you see their growth and progress. When athletes who struggle to produce in one season finally achieve a higher level of production, there is nothing better than their teammates acknowledging their contribution and progress. Athletes often acknowledge this growth by simply saying, "I see you," or "I feel you." It's a way of acknowledging their teammate matters and their growth is noticed.

Here are a few examples of ways to verbally recognize growth and progress in your spouse:

- "Dear, I just wanted to take a moment and let you know how appreciative I am that you _____. I know it was a sacrifice. It means so much to me."
- "Honey, it meant the world to me when you _____. I see you are really trying. I love you."
- "Hey, I wanted to tell you I noticed that you _____. It really made my day. Great job. Thanks."

Notice that in all the examples above, there is not just a simple acknowledgment that something changed or that growth occurred. There is also the explanation of how it made you feel to experience the change. When we express to our spouses that their actions give us a sense of happiness and delight or bring us a sense of gratitude, it makes them want to bring out that sense of elation and bliss more often. We all win in our marriages when our spouses express their happiness instead of their disappointment.

CELEBRATE

My (George's) father always taught me to find places that celebrate me and not simply tolerate me. People, especially our spouses, love to be celebrated. This cannot be overstated and expressed enough. While consistently criticizing or pointing out wrongs can be seen as negative and heading in the wrong direction, celebrating small and big wins can be the positive direction that many relationships are thirsting for daily. Acknowledging improvements or positive change is good, but it is only the start.

Celebrating goes beyond recognizing improvements. Celebrating says the improvement or finished task made a difference and brought impact to the team or game. When we are celebrated or when we celebrate others, it improves our relationships. Everyone wants to feel that their contribution and teamwork made an indelible mark on the team.

In a *Harvard Business Review* article, Whitney Johnson writes on the effects of celebrating in the workplace: "Celebrating small wins stimulates dopamine release in the brain, a feel-good chemical that reinforces the learning experience and strengthens our sense of connection to those we work with."[4] If celebrating wins helps strengthen connections in the workplace, shouldn't we work just as hard celebrating each other in our marriages and families? The ability to make our spouses feel good about what they bring to the table is a total game changer.

> *Moments of celebrating often lead to establishing a deeper bond, connection, and friendship.*

Sometimes it can be easier to celebrate the improvements or accomplishments of others outside our home than it is to celebrate our spouses or significant others. Many times, even our pets get more praise for doing something right than our spouses. You don't believe me? Pay attention to what you do the next time your pet sits or fetches on command or relieves themselves in the right place! We celebrate them by jumping, shouting, and praising them in high-pitched voices. Some of us even kiss them! We get so much more excited and animated over our two- and four-legged friends than we do about our spouses. Shouldn't we treat and celebrate our spouses better than our family pets?

Celebrations come in all types of sizes and expressions. Some celebrations can be as small as a quick high five or a fist bump while passing in the hallway. We could go one step further and plant a big, sloppy kiss on our spouse while giving them a warm embrace. Other times, celebrating could be preparing a special meal or taking them to their favorite restaurant. How spouses choose to celebrate will differ from couple to couple. Whatever you decide, find a way to cut out a few moments of criticism and do what the song says: "Accentuate the positive, eliminate the negative." Moments of celebrating often lead to establishing a deeper bond, connection, and friendship.

FRIENDSHIP HELPS STRENGTHEN CONNECTION

All love and deep connection should be built on the solid foundation of friendship. God has called us to leave others and cleave or be glued to the spouse we chose, and friendship is a part of that deep connection and commitment. Far too many couples start out having the spiritual glue that connects them in marriage by God but, over time, get disillusioned with marriage, thinking only God is responsible for keeping them together no matter what. No. Our part is to continue cleaving and bonding and being glued to each other, and friendship is a healthy part of that process.

Marital bonds that once held you together can be tested and worn in every season. That's why we must do our part and continue pouring into the relationship and sowing into the friendship. Wedding ceremonies often include a hint of caution: "What God has put together let no man or woman separate or pull away" (see Matt. 19:6). We must do our part.

Establishing a healthy friendship is one of the foundational ways we do our part. Without friendship, any serious relationship will collapse and erode over time. Friendship can make or break marital bonds throughout each season of a marriage. Just as we go through changes in weather with each season, we go through seasonal changes in our marriages. Each season—just like fall, winter, spring, and summer—brings with it changes in temperature in our relationships.

In some seasons, like spring, everything seems to be vibrant and in full bloom. Then summer comes, and it seems like we spend endless days doing everything together and enjoying each other. When autumn hits, things in our lives often start to drop like the leaves that fall from the trees, and change appears unavoidable. And then we all need to prepare for the changes that winter brings, when things are simply too cold and too hard and isolation can set in. No matter how we try to prepare for them, different seasons only come with more changes.

Many times, handling the changing seasons of a marriage is like dealing with weather-related seasonal changes. We simply prepare and respond to the change with the understanding that another season is around the corner. When you find yourself in an unpredictable season of change in marriage, don't panic. Instead, know another season is coming. You'll experience times when you sense less passion and desire, when things aren't blooming as much as they did in the past, when you hit a hard season and find yourself isolating, and when you feel the love and admiration are falling. During these times, please remember that one of the important things that keeps us steady when change is all around us is our friendship and bond in our marriage.

How can you maintain a solid friendship in a healthy marriage? One way is by continuing to cultivate a genuine bond and investing in developing a deep friendship. In marriage and long-term relationships, couples can sometimes fall into the routine of family life, work, chores, and the inevitable relationship autopilot. As couples desire to have a game plan for their marriage and create a winning team, looking at how sports teams build deeper bonds and chemistry can perhaps help couples see the bigger picture. Building deeper bonds and growing team chemistry are key to the success of the team. On sports teams, strengthening friendships often has big payoffs. It can mean the difference between simply playing together or winning it all as one team.

We are not saying that there is an equal comparison between friendship in marriage and friendship on sports teams. But there are a few similarities that are key to keeping couples active in developing their friendship and chemistry to win in their marriage. Remember, winning and success are the goals of every team, especially a marriage team.

Building deeper bonds and growing team chemistry are key to the success of the team.

SEVEN C'S OF STRENGTHENING FRIENDSHIP ON ANY TEAM

To help you win in marriage, we have compiled a list of seven key building blocks that couples, just like sports teams, can use to build friendship and closer relational bonds. To make this list easier to remember, each building block starts with the letter C:

1. COMMITMENT

Anything worth having deserves a certain level of commitment and focus, especially when you are a team that desires to win. Each teammate must decide on day one that the end goal of winning is achieved through a group effort of being all in. When teammates question the commitment of the other players, it often works against creating a winning mindset and culture. Conversely, when teammates trust the commitment of each person on the team, a tighter bond of friendship grows.

The same is true in a healthy marriage. Each spouse needs to be able to trust that the marriage will always be the priority for their partner and that fighting to win in their marriage will always be paramount.

2. CONSISTENCY

Winning teams bond quickly when teammates can count on each other to display a level of consistency in performance for the sake of the team. Consistency is about follow-through, attitude, focus, and effort. It outweighs promises and hype. Consistency says you can count on me on and off the field.

In marriage, consistency strengthens friendship and trust as spouses can count on each other to show up with their best game, love, and devotion in every season. When your spouse sees your consistency in love, forgiveness, service, and commitment to a happy and healthy marriage and family, your bond of connection grows.

3. COLLABORATION

Great teams win together because they recognize a need for each teammate's talents, voice, skills, passions, and energy. It is often said in sports that there is no *I* in *team*. Teams cannot win with just one person doing it all. Greatness happens in teams that know how to foster a sense of collaboration and cooperation. The bonds between teammates grow exponentially when players can sense that each person has their back and will always have the team's best interests in mind.

The same is true in marriage. Great marriages are built on the cooperation and collaboration of both spouses bringing their best game to the union.

4. CULTURE

Building the right culture on any team is critically important. A team's "culture" speaks of its vision, values, accountability, work ethic, trust, and appreciation. Winning cultures establish their "why," or purpose, for everything they do and stand for. When the wrong culture is established on a team, it often works against the desire to win together. For example, when a team culture seeks to build the team around one person or personality and not the strengths and gifts of the entire team, a wrong culture can be established.

When spouses establish and respect a healthy and well-thought-out culture in their marriage, it fosters great trust and connection in the family. For couples of faith, we have a cultural blueprint that we can follow in our marriages and families. God gives us a way and standard by which to treat each other and grow together through His Word, the Holy Bible.

5. CONVICTION

When sports teams come out of the tunnel to enter the stadium, they must have a resolute conviction that defeat is not an option. It matters not who the rival or opponent is; what matters most is the team's conviction that they will play, sacrifice, and win together. A team that plays with this conviction can and will make it through anything together.

The same is true in marriage. Both spouses must believe that they, as two, are better than one and that they can get through anything together. There are so many things that test a couple's resolve in marriage. Having the right mindset and conviction from the start helps any couple develop and have a successful game plan for marriage.

6. COMMUNICATION

Great sports teams are great communicators. Verbal communication is key in calling the right plays, communicating where the areas of vulnerabilities lie, and motivating the team during every season. Nonverbal communication is equally important when facing rivals. Teams communicate nonverbally through body language, attitude, and endurance to fight through tough moments of pain or loss.

The same is true in marriage. Great marriages are built on good communication, both verbal and nonverbal. Spouses must understand how to speak each other's love languages. Healthy and effective communication gives couples a great chance of winning their home game.

7. CELEBRATION

Winning sports teams know how to celebrate together. Celebrating is a part of winning and overcoming. That's why we called this chapter "Victory Mondays." Taking time to pause and celebrate together gives teams more appreciation for fighting and winning together.

In marriage, embracing moments of celebrating wins, big and small, gives us a deeper connection for the long haul. Victory Mondays in marriage bring life, laughter, and deep appreciation for our spouse and family.

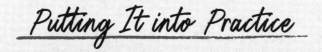

QUESTIONS

1. What impacted you most from this chapter, and why?

2. What are two small and two big wins that you and your spouse need to pause and celebrate this week?

3. How can you acknowledge and celebrate the areas where your spouse has experienced personal growth?

4. In what specific ways can you and your spouse work on strengthening your friendship?

5. Choose one of the seven C's and explain why it's important to you.

6. Complete the following sentences with your spouse in mind. After you finish, take a moment to share your responses with your spouse.

> I am grateful for ...
> Thank you for ...
> I admire ...
> I appreciate ...
> I value ...
> I'm blessed to have ...
> Your kindness in _____ has not gone unnoticed.
> Your support with _____ means the world to me.

COUPLE'S ACTIVITY: CONNECTION CONVERSATION

Institute a consistent Victory Monday tradition as a couple to celebrate both the major achievements and the smaller triumphs that you achieve together. Couples who integrate regular Victory Mondays into their relationship are likely to enjoy increased marital satisfaction, as well as more frequent moments of joy and mutual appreciation.

Building and nurturing your friendship throughout your marriage is crucial for long-term success and happiness. This activity includes some questions that you can explore together to deepen your friendship. The goal is to help you strengthen your friendship, emotional connection, and overall relationship satisfaction. Continue to pursue questions like these to deepen your friendship through every season.

- What's your idea of a fun day, and why?
- What are you most excited about in our relationship during this season, and why is it important to you?
- What are your dreams for yourself and our relationship in the future?
- What do I need to know most about you right now?
- When have you felt closest to me, and what made that moment special?
- What would you do if fear and finances were not an obstacle, and why?
- What are your favorite memories of us together? Plan a time to re-create similar experiences.

In addition to those questions, here are a few more ideas on ways you can grow closer. Sharing and doing activities together is also good for strengthening friendship and connection.

1. Share with your spouse what two strengths they bring to the relationship and how it makes you feel to have those things in your life.
2. Share with your spouse your top three favorite love songs and why they are your favorites. (For extra credit, sing some of the lyrics.) Find time to listen to your combined list of favorite love songs together. Work together to start building your love song playlist.
3. Brainstorm and share ideas for a new experience you can do together that takes you outside your comfort zone. Plan it.

PRAYER POINTS TO CONSIDER

ACTION ITEMS
(What steps, actions, or decisions do you need to make or take?)

TIME-OUT

For further insights and practical tips from this chapter, take a time-out and view our short bonus video, "Time-Out: Victory Mondays," using this link or QR code:

https://davidccook.org/access

Access code: GamePlan

Chapter 8

TEAMWORK IN CONFLICT

The real art of conversation is not only to say the right thing in the right place, but, far more difficult still, to leave unsaid the wrong thing at the tempting moment.
Lady Dorothy Nevill

Any team that desires to win will ultimately have to deal with conflicts that arise along the journey. Conflicts are natural when you bring people together and place them on a team. They arise from all sorts of reasons, but one of the main reasons is our differences: differences of upbringing, cultures, values, egos, history, experiences, likes, and dislikes, and the list goes on and on. We wish simply having a common goal of winning was all that was needed to become a great team. In reality, we must overcome our issues and conflicts when they arise, both on and off the field, to get to the winner's circle.

It is no different for two individuals who desire to win in marriage; they must overcome times of conflict when big and petty issues arise. Conflicts must be dealt with correctly and appropriately, or they can derail the love and happiness of any marriage team. We know this firsthand as our different ways of trying to resolve conflict almost caused our love to derail at the start of our marriage.

During our first year as husband and wife, one huge conflict quickly escalated. Ironically, we cannot remember why we were arguing in the first place. Have you been there before? Although we both at different times tried to resolve the conflict in our own way, neither one of us appreciated the other's approach, and we ultimately had an explosion that almost got out of control. You see, my (George's) way of resolving the conflict was to "humbly" try to point out where Tondra was wrong and how she could have done a better job. In my mind, I was simply showing her how not to get us in this heated place again, but it was not the right time or place to do this.

Tondra's way of resolving the conflict was not dealing with it in the moment and simply shutting down. She was unlike me in that she wanted to process it quietly in her head. She was an internal processor, and I was an overcommunicator. The more I talked, the angrier Tondra became. As Tondra walked away from me to get some space to think, I walked closely behind, trying to express my point of view from room to room. It was indeed a clash of the titans. Suddenly Tondra hurled the TV remote across the room to get me to stop talking and to leave her alone. She barely missed my head. The remote was not like today's slim, flimsy remote controls with rounded edges. Instead, it was built like a solid Sherman tank with pointed edges like that of a ninja star. She threw the remote so fast I was sure it stuck in the wall before it crashed on the floor behind the couch.

As any man would, I felt totally disrespected by my wife's effort to bludgeon me with the remote. Feeling belittled, I kindly asked her to pick up the remote. She rejected my offer several times, and I was obliged to carefully lift her over the back of the couch until she picked the remote up. After a few moments of struggle, she finally came up with the remote, and I thought I had finally won. Until I heard her on the phone with 9-1-1! This was not our best moment. We both were fighting to resolve our conflict in our own way instead of as a team.

UNITY IN CONFLICT

Thank goodness, one of us found a Scripture that taught us there was a better way to handle each other apart from our old ways of communicating and doing things. The new way was God's way. We both were fighting so hard to bring our way from our upbringings into our marriage that we failed to ask God what His way was for our marriage. His way was simply the way of unity that would usher in a new culture and dynamic in our marriage and home that we desperately needed, but we were too focused on our own agenda. Here is the Scripture that helped us: "How good and pleasant it is when God's people live together in unity! ... For there the LORD bestows his blessing, even life forevermore" (Ps. 133:1, 3).

This passage teaches us that unity in a marriage or a relationship should be an essential goal or focal point. Every married couple should desire and work toward unity and teamwork throughout the relationship. This concept of unity is not just a relational goal but a God-given inclination placed on our hearts through God's Word. This text informs us that when there is unity and togetherness, there is also an atmosphere of happiness, pleasure, delight, and harmony.

We can continually grow in unity as we deepen our understanding of one another and forge an increasingly cohesive bond. Unity brings a sense of collaboration, support, and mutual respect that cannot happen when we are concerned with only our selfish ways and interests. Tondra and I eventually learned that for the sake of the team we had to come up with a better approach to communicating in moments when we were feeling frustrated and not seeing eye to eye.

> *Everyone has to give up something for the sake of unity.*

Instead of allowing things to get out of hand like they did when Tondra threw the remote at me, we had to agree to do things differently. I had to allow Tondra time to think and process and give up my need to get things off my chest in the heat of the moment. At the same time, Tondra had to learn to process more quickly and not stay in her head for as long. Our new way of processing and communicating enabled our marriage team to experience unity instead of constant division and fighting to have things our own selfish way. Everyone has to give up something for the sake of unity. Our new way brought more happy times of harmony and delight.

Every sports team that desires to win together must have unity and teamwork. Teams are made up of individuals, but those individuals must come together to find a way to win. Mere talent is not enough. Grit, sacrifice, and determination can take you only so far. Teams win when they find a sense of teamwork and unity that will weather the storms of losses, injuries, or setbacks. Study any professional team that has won a championship, and you will sense a culture of teamwork, unity, and togetherness.

If unity is a key ingredient and building block in winning teams, conflict can be the culprit that threatens a team's ultimate success, especially in marriage. However, not all conflict is bad. I know that might seem odd to hear, but conflict or disagreements that end with a deeper understanding of your spouse or improved collaboration that helps the marriage can be good in the long run.

> *Every married couple should desire and work toward unity and teamwork throughout the relationship.*

For the first few years of our marriage, Tondra and I were desperately trying to figure each other out. Like most newlywed couples, we thought we knew each other, but getting married and living with your spouse shows you just how much more you need to learn about a person. It was in our moments of conflict or disagreement that we got a true sense of knowing what each of us liked and disliked, how we were wired, and how we made decisions.

One of the conflicts that we encountered in our early years was a result of Tondra's independent ways, which she unknowingly brought into our new marriage. As a single woman, going shopping after work and hanging out with her girlfriends was a very normal part of her everyday life. She did not have to check in with anyone and let them know where she was after work or when she'd be home—all typical things of a single woman.

As a new husband, I wanted to know when I arrived home that my wife would be there or that she would at least call to let me know when she would be coming home. I desperately tried to let her know my love for her and my desire to make sure she was safe. I wanted to know where she was just in case something happened, and I also wanted to plan for our time together. But she did not see it the way I did and thought I was trying to control her.

This led to a few moments of "intense fellowship" for sure, but thank God, we learned from these conflicts. Over time, instead of thinking that I didn't trust her or was trying to control her, Tondra saw my heart as a source of protection and deep care. I, too, learned that Tondra's best self often came out after she had time to decompress and unwind a little. What could have continued to be a conflict that divided us became something that gave us a deeper understanding of each other.

CONFLICT IGNITES OUR TRIGGERS

While not all conflict is bad for a marriage, unhealthy, unresolved, and unaddressed conflict can throw a relationship into a death spiral. Conflicts can ignite personal triggers in all of us. These triggers often arise from old, ingrained patterns and mindsets that we learn over time but are not willing to part ways with easily. Many times, they are hard to recognize because they are a part of who we are and what makes us tick. We can become triggered when we sense someone is trying to change us, especially if we are set in our ways. And we all know that our spouse holds hidden secrets that push our buttons with just the right word, tone, or phrase. Here are a few additional key ways that conflict can ignite our triggers.

OUR "RIGHTS" ARE VIOLATED

When we talk about "rights" in this section, we are not talking about a person's inalienable rights, as each person should be treated with honor, respect, and appreciation. When we discuss our "rights" here, we mean our "way." Sometimes as individuals, we think our way is the only and right way, and our way should be the only way because it's only right—right? And so, often in conflict, when our way (our rights) is not adhered to, we are triggered, and we fight for our way to be the normal way.

This way of thinking is simply not true and can be perceived as almost narcissistic, making a spouse seem somewhat like a dictator instead of a partner. There is no one-size-fits-all way to do marriage or family. Couples must figure out the best way for their marriage and family to work together throughout their marital relationship. No spouse should have a monopoly on how things will go in the relationship or family.

One gentleman said in a coaching session one day, "It's either my way or the highway." We told him if he wanted it his way that he simply had to go to Burger King. That hamburger chain's slogan at the time was "Have It Your Way." They have since updated their slogan to emphasize our point here even more: "You Rule." No spouse gets to rule or have it their way in marriage 100 percent of the time. We often hear the phrase "Happy wife, happy life," and it makes us cringe. This sentiment gives the impression that happiness in the home revolves solely around the wife. We prefer a different and a more well-rounded sentiment instead: "Happy spouse, happy house." So we have to be very careful not to be triggered when our "rights" are violated.

During the earlier years of our marriage when our kids were small, Tondra expected us to spend every Thanksgiving and Christmas at her mother's home since her mother was a single parent and Tondra had no siblings. However, I anticipated spending those holidays with my family, given my upbringing in a large, close-knit family. We both wanted to have it our way, but we could not be in two places at one time. Instead of fighting for our individual plans, we had to compromise and come up with a solution that would work for both of us. We decided to make a new tradition of spending most Christmas holidays at Tondra's mother's home and Thanksgivings at my parents' home and inviting Tondra's mother to attend. Those were some of the best times.

There is no one-size-fits-all way to do marriage or family.

OUR EXPECTATIONS ARE NOT MET

Often in marriages, a spouse can be triggered when their expectations are not met. In general, unmet expectations can lead to feeling let down and frustrated, which in turn can lead to anger and resentment. Marriage should be a safe place to discuss expectations, but all expectations should be talked about and agreed upon by both spouses.

That's why we teach that unspoken expectations are a recipe for being let down. Over the years during coaching sessions with couples, I (George) will hear one spouse say about the other spouse, "They should just get me. They should know what I want if they love me." My response is always, "Your spouse does not know or understand everything about you, especially those things that you have not communicated or revealed." Our spouses are not mind readers. Discussing expectations is key to not triggering each other.

A couple we were counseling had a big disagreement surrounding their expectations of celebrating each other's birthday. The wife grew up in a home in which her parents celebrated her birthday for an entire week. Each birthday week was ceremoniously celebrated by affectionately crowning her "princess of the week" and giving her gifts and treats. Her husband, on the other hand, was lucky to receive a card or gift to acknowledge his birthday each year. He grew up thinking birthdays were not a big deal. You can see where this is going, can't you?

During the first year of their marriage, the husband acknowledged his wife's birthday with a card and by singing "Happy Birthday." While he was extremely proud that he acknowledged her birthday, she was deeply hurt, as the celebration could not compare to what she was accustomed to growing up with her parents. As you can imagine, this issue caused quite a lively counseling session that lasted hours the following week. To be fair, they had not discussed expectations surrounding birthday celebrations. Needless to say, the husband has stepped up his game and goes all out for her birthday each year.

OUR HURTS CAUSE OFFENSE

Let's face it: Marriage, just like all relationships, is often accompanied by moments of unintentional hurt and pain. These moments of hurt trigger us and can reveal our insecurities and sensitive emotional areas from the past. This often leads us to react in ways that are not healthy or good for the relationship.

When hurts from the past trigger us to get offended, it can cause us to build walls of bitterness and resentment. Our encouragement to all married couples is to take the time that is needed and talk through past hurts and insecurities and try to get an understanding of things that may trigger your spouse. But don't stop at just talking. Dig deeper and seek the inner healing that each of us needs from the traumas and hurts from our past. Perhaps this can be done through praying with your pastor or seeking help from a counselor. Don't allow the pain of the past to trigger conflict in your marriage. Instead, guard your heart. Proverbs reminds us, "Above all else, guard your heart, for everything you do flows from it" (4:23).

OUR DIFFERENCES CAUSE DIVISION

When you stood in front of all your family and friends and declared your love for each other on that sacred day when you said, "I do," God knew two different people were coming together. It's actually the differences that probably drew you together and made you feel as though you could not live without each other. Our challenge is to not allow the differences to trigger us and bring unwanted tension. This causes us to fight and pulls us apart. Instead, we must fight for unity, even during times of conflict. Remember God calls us to unity (Ps. 133:1, 3), as unity is the place He commands His blessing. There will always be things that cause conflicts or disagreements. The question is not if conflict will arise but when will it arise.

When it does raise its menacing head, couples do much better settling conflicts when they have an agreed-upon set of "rules of engagement" so that World War III will not happen. The rules of engagement are agreed-upon guidelines that dictate how both spouses should interact with each other, especially in attempting to resolve conflict. Agreeing and committing to a clear set of rules of engagement helps maintain unity and peace.

Here are a few nonnegotiable rules of engagement that have helped us and countless other couples for many years.

RULE 1: REMEMBER YOU ARE ON THE SAME TEAM

We've mentioned this several times throughout this book, but it is critical to understand that you and your spouse are on the same team, especially during discussions about touchy subjects or during moments when it feels like you are enemies. At times, both Tondra and I have framed tough conversations with this phrase, and many times we will keep repeating it throughout our moments of disagreement to reassure the other that our intentions are pure. But we cannot just say it. We must mean it and treat our spouse as if they are indeed and will remain our teammate long after any conflict.

RULE 2: HONOR EACH OTHER

We are called to always honor our spouse, during good and not-so-good times. When we honor our spouse, especially during times of conflict, we simply care for our spouse's heart through respectful and loving means of communication. Many times, people want to let words fire out of their mouths regardless of whether they offend or injure someone else just to get their point across. A mentor once told us in a coaching session that the purpose of communication is to be heard, not just to let words fly aimlessly.

Words can be weapons of mass destruction that deepen the conflict, or they can bring clarity, peace, and resolution to both spouses. If we want our spouses to hear our hearts, we must start by honoring their hearts with respectful and loving communication. A pivotal Scripture that has served as our beacon, guiding us in how we love and honor each other through our communication, is 1 Corinthians 13:4–8:

> Love is patient, love is kind. It does not envy, it does not boast, it is not proud. It does not dishonor others, it is not self-seeking, it is not easily angered, it keeps no record of wrongs. Love does not delight in evil but rejoices with the truth. It always protects, always trusts, always hopes, always perseveres. Love never fails.

RULE 3: HANDLE WITH CARE

How we handle conflict directly impacts our marital satisfaction. We show our spouses we care for them through our words and actions. Effectively resolving conflict can strengthen your bond instead of allowing the conflict to tear you apart. Handling your spouse with care should be a priority, just as we would handle anything that we cherish and want to protect, like expensive technology gadgets, family pets, a new car, or delicate plants.

Anyone who knows me knows that I (George) highly prize the delicate succulent plants in my garden. I treat them like they are my babies, and there have been times that Tondra has caught me talking to them and showing them affection. I have one plant called a Madagascar palm. Its six-foot trunk is loaded with sharp thorns that make caring for it at times arduous and dangerous, and yet I handle it with tender loving care.

One day Tondra and I were teaching together on stage, and the topic of care for our spouse came up as a talking point. Tondra could not wait to tell the audience how tenderly and delicately I treated my Madagascar palm. It was a setup indeed. As she made fun of my love affair with my palm, she made a point to say, "Now, surely if George can care for a Madagascar palm with sharp spines, I know he should be able to handle me with care as his spouse on good or bad days." The same should be true in all relationships and marriages. We must prioritize our spouse with care and respect above all things.

A part of handling our spouse with care involves controlling our emotions. Controlling our emotions is a sign of maturity and should be one of the ultimate goals in how we treat our spouse. An emotionally mature person has self-control and should consider not only what they want to communicate but also how it might affect others, especially their spouse. It is critical to prioritize handling our spouse with care, especially when it comes to words and communication styles. The Bible gives us helpful tips and wisdom on controlling our words: "In the multitude of words sin is not lacking, but he who restrains his lips is wise" (Prov. 10:19 NKJV) and "My dear brothers and sisters, take note of this: Everyone should be quick to listen, slow to speak and slow to become angry" (James 1:19).

These verses let us know that handling our spouses with care is within our reach. We can control what we say and how we say it. Galatians 5:22–23 lets us know that self-control is a fruit of walking with the Holy Spirit and is critical in displaying God's character and love toward others. If we are having problems handling our spouse with care and practicing self-control with our words, we can simply ask God to help us be filled with His Spirit and be self-controlled in what we say and how we respond during times of conflict.

Don't be like Dr. David Bruce Banner, the lead character in *The Incredible Hulk* TV series. Throughout the series, although he is an ordinary man, he often reacts to stressful and heart-pounding situations by turning into the Incredible Hulk. The Incredible Hulk is a big, muscular green monster that represents Dr. Banner's out-of-control, angry nature. When special music started playing in the show, you always knew it was too late for him to keep his anger under control. Dr. Banner never could control the inner nature of the Incredible Hulk once his anger was triggered. We, on the other hand, can ask God for help or go seek practical help from a trusted counselor or relationship coach.

You don't have to turn into the Incredible Hulk in your relationship when things don't go your way. A practical way of trying to master self-control in communication in your relationship is learning to slow down and not react too quickly. For some of us, this is a novel concept as we've learned to be very reactionary in how we handle conflict. During sports programming, when there is a foul or a boundary is crossed, the referees employ a simple tool during the game that can help us out as couples. They use instant replay to slow the play down enough to see where the foul occurred or whether there was a foul at all. The emphasis here is slowing the action down enough to see what went wrong, how it occurred, and how to move forward.

The next time a conflict happens in your relationship, try slowing things down and practice pausing so you will not overreact and jump to conclusions. Instead of assuming your feelings have not deceived you, ask your spouse if what you interpreted from their comments is indeed what they said and intended. Asking clarifying questions can often get us back on the right track. Or perhaps call a time-out and give yourself a few moments to cool off before you continue with the conversation so you can think clearly and be less reactionary. Conflicts many times come in fast and hot. Learning to slow things down is essential to resolving conflict and not letting things get out of control.

We mentioned in chapter 4 that during moments of conflict, we say, "You are not my enemy." This is our key phrase to let the other person know that we need to take a moment and hit the reset button and that we are not the other's enemy. Once we go to our neutral corners, we've learned to calm down and start asking ourselves the right questions. We think of it as a time of introspection and reflection. We ask questions like "How did I contribute to the foul, problem, or disagreement?" and "What triggered me to say certain things?"

We ask ourselves these specific questions so that we don't simply blame each other for everything. Blaming is a quick way to ignite or reignite conflict. We look for ways of taking responsibility and owning our part of the conflict without placing all the blame on the other person. Taking these moments to simply walk away and reflect has revolutionized our responses to conflict over the years.

We encourage couples to have a "thermostat mentality" when it comes to handling their spouse with care. There is a big difference between a thermometer and a thermostat. A thermometer *reacts* to its environment and simply reads the specific temperature in the room. A thermostat, on the other hand, has the ability to *respond* to its environment by setting the temperature in the room. In handling conflict, don't simply react like a thermometer. Instead, be like the thermostat that responds to the conflict and sets the right temperature of handling with care.

RULE 4: FORGIVE LAVISHLY

As we've said before, conflict is inevitable in our relationships and marriages. Where there is unresolved conflict, we often find unforgiveness, disappointment, resentment, pain, and hurt. Our suggestion is to find a way to resolve conflicts as timely as possible and learn to move beyond the pain and disappointment. Don't stay stuck and continue rehearsing the conflict over and over. Instead, just like in sports, learn to turn the page quickly. Athletes know how to let mistakes go and have a short-term memory. The alternative is to let mistakes negatively affect the next play, game, or season. No one wants that. Learn to forgive lavishly.

Don't think we are saying moving beyond conflicts and painful moments or extending forgiveness is easy. We are not saying that in the least. Resolving conflicts and extending forgiveness can be some of the hardest things in marriage. And yet after thirty years of being married, we've learned time and time again that daily practice leads the way to growth and progress. If we practice forgiving daily, we will learn to get better and better at extending forgiveness and not staying stuck over time. On the other hand, if we rarely, if ever, practice forgiveness or extend grace to our spouse, then we set ourselves up to rehearse the problems and pain that conflicts bring with them.

When we suggest practicing forgiveness as a daily habit, we are simply suggesting looking to Christ for His love and power to forgive. Ephesians 4 tells us: "And be kind to one another, tenderhearted, forgiving one another, even as God in Christ forgave you" (v. 32 NKJV).

We can forgive others only when we remember that we've been forgiven much through our relationship with Christ. To forgive like a pro, we've got to turn to the GOAT (greatest of all time) who showed us the way. Christ was the greatest forgiver of all time as He taught us to forgive despite accusation, insult, or injury on the cross when He said, "Father, forgive them, for they do not know what they are doing" (Luke 23:34).

Some people think that extending forgiveness is a sign of weakness, but it is a sign of strength. Mahatma Gandhi once said, "The weak can never forgive. Forgiveness is the attribute of the strong."[1]

RULE 5: DON'T WEAPONIZE THE WORD DIVORCE

Individuals marry each other because they want to be lifelong partners and win together. They want a marriage that is built to last the most challenging and best of times. We don't know any couple who married with the sole purpose of ending it all and calling it quits. And yet sadly, many couples decide to end it all despite beginning with the best intentions. While not all marriages survive, couples who work together to build unity, trust, and a lifelong commitment can make it, especially if they avoid the urge to walk away or give up when times get tough.

One way of giving your marriage a fighting chance is to avoid weaponizing the word *divorce*. In military rules of engagement, all talks cease when there is talk of employing a deadly bomb. Just the mention of the word *divorce* can be a deadly bomb in your marriage. If couples bring up divorce, there is bound to be an erosion of trust and belief that each partner is working toward the same goal. When a spouse uses the possibility of divorce to threaten or punish the other spouse, it is like taking a chisel and destroying the masterpiece that God has so brilliantly designed. Please take our advice and agree to this rule of engagement.

One of the best ways to counterattack the feeling of giving up on your marriage is to show your spouse that you are in the fight with them to save your marriage, not seeking a way out every time there is a challenging moment or season. Often when partners bring up divorce, it is a sign that they need help resolving an issue or situation beyond their ability or know-how.

Most of our marital problems can be resolved if we seek the right help before it's too late. That is why we consistently tell couples not to drown in a sea of lifeguards. For couples who are willing to do the hard work, help abounds for their marriages and relationships. Much of that hard work begins when we confess that we need help and don't have all the answers.

> *If we want our spouses to hear our hearts, we must start by honoring their hearts with respectful and loving communication.*

In any relationship, there will be conflicts to resolve. Understanding how disagreements and misunderstandings often ignite our personal triggers is critical to responding and resolving conflict. Remembering the rules of engagement listed in this chapter (or coming up with your own list) can be a lifesaver as you and your spouse tackle tough conversations.

Putting It into Practice

QUESTIONS

1. What impacted you most from this chapter, and why?

2. Identify two or three things that have tried to come against your unity as a couple. Have those issues been resolved? If not, try doing this chapter's Couple's Activity, which we've designed to help couples resolve conflict.

3. Think of a time when you successfully resolved a conflict in your marriage. How did resolving the conflict improve your relationship and make you stronger as a couple?

4. Name a time when your partner insisted on having things go their way (like a customer at Burger King), and explain how that made you feel.

5. What are some unexpressed expectations that have contributed to discord in your marriage?

COUPLE'S ACTIVITY: UNITY IN CONFLICT
RULES OF ENGAGEMENT

Create your unique set of "rules of engagement." Remember, agreeing and committing to a clear set of rules of engagement helps you maintain unity and peace, especially as you attempt to resolve conflicts. Your rules of engagement can come from this chapter, or you can add rules that you believe would be beneficial to incorporate into your marriage.

CONFLICT-RESOLUTION PLAYBOOK

The goal of this activity is to slow conflict down and decrease the reactivity surrounding it for easier resolution. Practice utilizing the steps of the conflict-resolution playbook with a minor conflict, such as how to get to places on time or where to take your next vacation. The objective is to familiarize yourselves with the playbook steps by addressing a simple conflict and avoiding anything overly triggering. Choosing a conflict that allows you to practice the steps comfortably will reinforce your ability to navigate disagreements constructively.

1. Acknowledge and agree there is a conflict that needs focused time to resolve. This agreement aligns you as a team against the problem rather than reinforcing the idea that the other person is the problem.

2. Schedule an agreed-upon time to discuss the conflict. This ensures both spouses come ready to work toward a solution in a logical way focused on the same goal. Remove all distractions for this planned time.

Resolution meeting time and date: _____

3. Diffuse the emotion by actively listening to and validating each person's position and point of view. Take turns and set a timer. This portion of the meeting needs to be limited to thirty minutes (fifteen minutes per person).

Remember to keep the big picture in mind, maintain honor and respect, exercise self-control, and stay calm. If you feel yourself escalating during this section, then communicate with your spouse that you need to take a break, and the other spouse needs to allow that to happen. Allow no more than thirty minutes for the break. If a longer time is needed, then reschedule the meeting for the next day. Agree on a time to resume the meeting.

To help each person to focus when their spouse is sharing, note the following prompts.

My husband's point of view: _____

Why is this perspective important to him?

What feelings are associated with his point of view?

My wife's point of view: _____

Why is this perspective important to her?

What feelings are associated with her point of view?

4. Make sure you are working to define and solve the same problem.

For example: One spouse may think the conflict is about spending too much money on shopping while the other spouse thinks the conflict is about spending time together and feeling alone. Shopping fills the void. One is a financial problem, and the other is a relationship problem. Even though the topic is about shopping, the problem they are trying to solve is different.

Husband's definition of the problem: _____

Wife's definition of the problem: _____

Agree on what problem you are resolving: _____

5. Brainstorm possible solutions. Both people contribute ideas to solve the problem. No judging each other's ideas. List all the possibilities. Discuss and evaluate each possible solution.

a. _____
_____

b. _____
_____

c. _____
_____

d. _____
_____

e. _____
_____

6. Agree on a solution. Pick one of the solutions to try. This process is where sacrifice and compromise are necessary. Each spouse must give up something for unity to take place. No one gets to have it completely their way.

Write down the solution:

7. Take responsibility. Determine what each person needs to commit to and sacrifice to implement the new solution. Remember, you are a team working toward a common goal.

Husband's responsibility: _____

Wife's responsibility: _____

8. Schedule a follow-up conversation (date) _____
(time) _____ **to discuss these questions:**

How effective is the new solution?

What needs to be adjusted?

PRAYER POINTS TO CONSIDER

ACTION ITEMS
(What steps, actions, or decisions do you need to make or take?)

# TIME-OUT

For further insights and practical tips from this chapter, take a time-out and view our short bonus video, "Time-Out: Teamwork in Conflict," using this link or QR code:

https://davidccook.org/access
Access code: GamePlan

Chapter 9

TIPS FOR TACKLING TOUGH CONVERSATIONS

Communication does not always occur naturally, even among a tight-knit group of individuals. Communication must be taught and practiced in order to bring everyone together as one.

Coach Mike Krzyzewski

In football, a tackle is the effort to stop the opponent from advancing down the field to score a touchdown. The opponent in your marriage is not your spouse; the tough issues that threaten your forward progress to winning in your relationship are the "enemies." The ability to tackle difficult issues in your relationship is essential to an effective marriage game plan. Tackling tough issues requires tough conversations. The reason some conversations are so challenging is because they surround what we like to call "hot topics." Certain topics are "hot" because they spark tension between the two members of the relationship.

Typical hot topics for most couples include work schedules, parenting, in-laws, finances, sex, household roles, social media, opposite-sex friendships, time management, and fertility challenges. You will have even more specific hot topics unique to your relationship. For your relationship to thrive, you need to be able to tackle tough conversations. Couples face so many challenges that threaten to divide them and break them up. They may find it difficult to address these issues, but they're a part of life.

Avoiding tough conversations creates division, disconnection, and isolation in a relationship. Couples avoid tough conversations for many reasons. First off, facing the issues is difficult and sometimes scary if you don't know how to handle them effectively. You may not know how or when to bring up a sore topic or what words to say. You may feel ill-equipped to handle the response you'll get, or maybe you think it's helpful to always get along and you want to have only good times. It is a fantasy to expect perpetual harmony and only blissful moments in marriage. Ignoring difficult conversations won't make them vanish; instead, the challenging issues tend to grow bigger.

One of the true hallmarks of a healthy relationship is the ability to navigate tough conversations in a way that builds safety and trust. In fact, tackling difficult conversations in a healthy way brings unity, connection, closeness, and the greatest relational reward, intimacy. To achieve intimacy, you must be willing to be vulnerable and transparent.

> *Ignoring difficult conversations won't make them vanish; instead, the challenging issues tend to grow bigger.*

VULNERABILITY AND TRANSPARENCY

A couple cannot have true intimacy without vulnerability and transparency. Vulnerability is the state of being exposed, expressing the sides of yourself you are least confident or certain of.[1]

Vulnerability is very scary because it means putting yourself in a position where your spouse can hurt you but trusting that they will not. Many people mishandle tough conversations in an effort to protect themselves from the pain of being vulnerable. When you operate out of the fear of being hurt, you put up walls between you and your spouse. However, not only do the walls keep you from feeling pain, but they also block you from feeling love. You cannot have it both ways.

You cannot pick and choose which feelings to keep and which feelings to throw away. To feel or not to feel, that is the question. If you want love in your life, you have to be willing to feel hurt and pain. You must be ready and willing to take the good and the bad, the bitter and the sweet. This is why it takes courage to be vulnerable.

Transparency is slightly different from vulnerability, but it adds a very important element to the mix. Transparency is being open, honest, and authentic in your relationship. Transparency and vulnerability are the wonder twins of relationships; they go together. Transparency without vulnerability lacks compassion and can come across as cold or brutal. You may have heard the term *brutal honesty*. Being brutally honest means speaking the truth in harsh, hurtful, and insensitive ways. This works against creating trust and safety, two critical elements needed for vulnerability in a relationship. Vulnerable honesty, on the other hand, is about speaking the truth with love, respect, and consideration. In both ways the truth is spoken, but one fosters an environment of trust and safety, and one shuts down communication and fosters division and disconnection.

UNHEALTHY COPING MECHANISMS

Developing a vulnerable and transparent marriage is easier said than done because the pain of past hurt causes individuals to develop unhealthy coping mechanisms to protect themselves. These unhealthy coping mechanisms are maladaptive behaviors or actions that prevent you from adjusting to what's needed in your relationship.[2] Addressing difficult issues will require you to tackle these unhealthy coping mechanisms. Some of the most common maladaptive relational behaviors are listed in the following paragraphs.

AVOIDANCE AND DENIAL

Avoidance and denial take place when someone ignores or suppresses stressful emotions because these emotions feel overwhelming.[3] The person's goal is to protect against the emotional impact of situations or tough conversations. For example, a wife may be expressing her feeling of hurt or disappointment about something her husband did or said, and the husband's response may be to focus on trying to solve the problem, intellectualize about the facts while ignoring the emotion, or dismiss her emotions all together, viewing them as dramatic or as an overreaction. Another example of how avoidance or denial may show up is if a husband feels put down by his wife but allows her to continue to criticize him without responding. Avoidance and denial can show up as apathy or a lack of interest or concern.

BLAMING AND DEFLECTION

With blaming and deflection, the goal is to not take personal responsibility, to redirect the focus, blame, or criticism away from oneself to preserve one's self-image or avoid negative consequences, such as guilt, failure, or shame.[4] For example, a husband shares his need to have sex more often, and the wife responds that she does everything with the kids and house and that he should not ask more of her when he doesn't help her out at all. In this scenario, the husband's failures become the focus and the wife suggests the problem is the husband's own fault.

PEOPLE-PLEASING

People-pleasing is when someone neglects themselves to be agreeable and appease their spouse.[5] The goal is to feel more secure in the relationship and earn approval and acceptance from their spouse. They will do whatever it takes to diffuse conflict to protect themselves against being abandoned or rejected or feeling like a burden. For example, when a husband expresses negative feelings, such as disagreement or disappointment, the wife may agree with whatever he says just to avoid an argument. Even though she may disagree with him or have a different perspective, need, or opinion, she will not share it. Another example of how people-pleasing may show up is a wife who feels unappreciated, neglected, and resentful of all her self-sacrificing and self-neglect, who feels exhausted from overextending herself to make everyone else happy and meet their needs.

PASSIVE-AGGRESSIVENESS

Passive-aggressiveness is indirectly expressing one's anger, negative feelings, problems, or disagreements in a way that undermines the other person instead of directly and openly talking about these feelings.[6] This may show up as giving your spouse the silent treatment, refusing to share your thoughts and feelings even when asked, or sharing with other people instead of your spouse. It's a way of punishing your partner and making them feel uncomfortable. Other passive-aggressive behaviors are sarcasm, eye-rolling, stubbornness, moodiness, hostile humor, and hypercriticism.

AGGRESSION

Aggression is intense, uncontrolled, excessive anger that is unprofitable. Examples of aggressive behaviors include hitting, kicking, pushing, throwing things, destroying things, stomping, name-calling, yelling, bullying, and intimidation.[7] Aggression doesn't have to be violent to cause harm. Nonviolent aggression can still lead to negative outcomes and cause verbal and psychological harm.

ISOLATION

Isolation is withdrawing, shutting down, or shutting out your spouse. A person who is isolating wants to distance themselves from distressing feelings, such as fear, anxiety, stress, or frustration, not necessarily from their spouse.[8] For example, a spouse may refuse to talk or answer questions, ignore their spouse completely, give them the silent treatment, and make no eye contact.

EXCESSIVE SCREEN TIME

Excessive screen time is an attempt to numb oneself or escape real life by absorbing technology.[9] Social media is increasingly showing up more and more in divorce proceedings. An example of this is when a spouse creates an alternate imaginary world, participating in virtual relationships or online groups instead of addressing real-life issues or working on their marriage.

All these coping mechanisms prevent you from engaging authentically in your relationship. They may seem authentic to you because they have become so ingrained in your subconscious that they happen automatically, without you even deciding to respond that way. The first step to learning a new, healthier coping mechanism is becoming aware of and acknowledging the unhealthy coping mechanisms. Then, practice slowing down your automatic response by recognizing when it shows up in your interactions, and give your spouse permission to let you know when they see it as well. Next, replace the bad habit with a healthier response that aligns with your goal of having true intimacy in your relationship.

This process is not easy, and it takes time; these changes will not happen overnight. It took many years to ingrain the unhealthy patterns, and it will take time to undo them. Be patient with yourself and celebrate your progress along the way. Because this process is not easy, you may need to seek professional help from a licensed therapist or a relationship coach. Please don't allow maladaptive behaviors and actions to keep you from having healthy relationships and getting the love you want and need.

Vulnerability and transparency give each member of the relationship the ability to be fully known and accepted, which in turn deepens their love and connection to each other. This is the only way to experience unconditional love and acceptance. Intimacy is achieved when you can be authentic and share your true thoughts and feelings with your spouse and in return receive safety, understanding, and acceptance.

> *When you operate out of the fear of being hurt, you put up walls between you and your spouse. However, not only do the walls keep you from feeling pain, but they also block you from feeling love.*

Many people never learned the skills necessary to tackle tough conversations in the home where they grew up. Others have seen the destruction that's caused when it's not done right. Being able to address challenging issues effectively is critical if you want to grow the deeper roots of safety, trust, and intimacy. We know it's not easy or fun to tackle tough topics in your relationship. In fact, sometimes couples try to avoid these conversations as much as possible.

George grew up in a household where they could say whatever was on their minds directly, without tact. There was no sugarcoating their words. I, on the other hand, didn't learn anything better. I grew up in a household where there was either extreme silent treatment with tension so thick you could cut it with a knife or explosive communication once the silence could no longer be held. As a couple, we were ill-equipped for navigating tough conversations; in fact, those conversations went very poorly. Or we would stay silent and walk on eggshells. But inevitably, one of us would say or do something that would ignite pent-up emotions and begin another poorly held conversation. It was a very destructive, ineffective cycle that had to be broken if we were to make our marriage work.

NIP IT IN THE BUD

On the football field, the objective of tackling is to halt the opposing team's forward progress. Similarly, for couples, it's crucial to stop tough conversations from escalating and getting out of control. It is best to deal with difficult topics as quickly as possible. Delaying challenging conversations, no matter why or how you feel about the topic, can make things worse. When you don't deal with an issue, the tension can escalate, causing things to be compounded or get out of control. Delaying a conversation only makes it harder to have one.

When things are neglected, it causes breakdowns. Maintenance is always easier to manage than a full-out breakdown. Think about your car: getting regular oil changes and tire rotations is recommended. It is truly inconvenient and time-consuming to handle and keep up with the maintenance, but it is not as inconvenient as blowing up your car engine or blowing out your tire, causing a car accident. These types of breakdowns come with a lot more frustration, loss, and cost. Avoiding hard conversations with your spouse actually makes things worse and harder to overcome. Avoidance causes things to build up and grow bigger and bigger.

Early on in our marriage, I (Tondra) oversaw the finances because I was a banker. We were going through some financial hardships when George was in graduate school, and I would borrow money from our savings to cover the shortage in our household finances. I intended to put it back, but it created a cycle; the savings deficit continued to mount until I could not replace what was borrowed. I realized I had wiped out all our savings and we were definitely without a safety net. This situation was created because I tried to avoid having a difficult conversation about our finances, but it made things a thousand times worse.

My fear, embarrassment, and shame kept me from having the conversation, and all the while we were digging the financial hole deeper and deeper. There is no way around having tough conversations in marriage because eventually things will come to the surface, and it won't be possible to hide them or put them off any longer. Why not talk about it sooner rather than later?

When you don't nip a problem in the bud, you leave room for each of you to create your own narrative or draw your own conclusion about what's going on. When this happens, you will react and respond to each other based on these distorted narratives. For example, a husband might think his wife doesn't like his mother because she gets upset whenever his mother wants to visit. The wife's narrative can be her husband does not respect her as his wife when it comes to his mom. Then, every time the mom wants to come for a visit, the couple gets into explosive arguments regarding her visit. When you nip it in the bud and have the tough conversation, you allow your spouse the opportunity to fill in the blanks and share their point of view and perspective. This is more effective than both of you reacting to made-up stories or assumptions.

Another reason to nip it in the bud is to prevent emotions from getting blown out of proportion, causing unnecessary hurts and disagreements. When things are allowed to fester, it's like a teapot reaching its boiling point and blowing its top. When you don't get to the bottom of things quickly, you run the risk of piling on more hurt, confusion, and disagreement. This gives room for things to be said that you might later regret; however, your spouse may not be able to forget. When this pile-on happens, it breeds reactiveness and sensitivity surrounding the conversation, creating a lot more things to dig through before you can even address the original tough conversation. This makes the issue seem even more daunting, giving even more reasons to avoid having the conversation. Not addressing the issue is not the answer; avoidance only creates a never-ending cycle that will slowly unravel the connection and closeness you once felt. You have got to put on your "big girl and big boy pants" and have the conversation.

FINDING THE RIGHT WORDS TO SAY

How to have a tough conversation is just as important as having the conversation. First, find the right words to say. Being reckless with your words is not operating in wisdom and maturity. It takes self-control to be measured in your words. Words reflect what's in your heart. Therefore, make sure your heart has not grown bitter or hardened toward your spouse. If it has, then ask

God to help you release whatever you have been harboring in your heart. The Bible says, "Let the words of my mouth and the meditation of my heart be acceptable in your sight, O LORD, my rock and my redeemer" (Ps. 19:14 ESV). Just as it is important to make sure your words and heart are pleasing to God, it's equally important for your words and heart to be right when tackling tough conversations with your spouse.

Another way to soften your heart toward your spouse is to meditate on what your spouse has done right or what's going right in your relationship. When you fixate on what's going wrong or what your spouse is doing wrong, it gives you an overall negative view of your spouse and your relationship. This, in turn, causes your heart to harden toward them, which can lead to negativity coming from your heart through your words and actions. Not being able to find the right words is a heart issue that needs to be addressed.

Here are some doable, time-tested, proven techniques to help you find the right words to tackle tough conversations daily.

START OFF POSITIVELY

Share with your spouse what's going well. This is your chance to affirm your spouse. As mentioned earlier, it takes five positive comments to balance out one negative comment.[10] To start off positively, you must think before you speak; it might be helpful to write out your thoughts first. Sometimes when we don't know the main points of what we want our spouse to know and hear, we can say a lot of things that are not well-thought-out. This could lead to saying the wrong things, at the wrong time, in the wrong way, and triggering an emotional reaction.

Starting off positively requires you to calm down before trying to have a conversation about a tough topic. Take a time-out to gather your thoughts and level off your emotions. Emotional reactions can trigger a fight-or-flight response, which means the part of your brain that houses self-control, logic, and problem-solving shuts down and surviving the emotional threat becomes the goal.[11] This causes us to say hurtful things in the moment that we can't take back, which triggers your spouse's defensiveness or their fight-or-flight response as well. Nothing productive is going to come from a conversation like this. According to the research of Dr. John Gottman, 96 percent of the time you can predict the outcome of a conversation based on the first three minutes.[12] His research reveals how a conversation starts predicts how it will end. If it starts harshly, it will end harshly.

TAKE OUT ANY NEGATIVELY CHARGED WORDS

This is why writing out your thoughts first is helpful: you can read your ideas and edit them by taking out or rewording anything negatively charged. Remember, the goal of communication is to be heard and understood. Having negatively charged words works against that goal because when someone feels attacked, they go into defense mode. Defense mode causes the person to focus on themselves instead of what you are saying and how it affects you. Negatively charged words are usually used to strike an emotional chord with the person listening, which can become a "hot button" in the conversation.

When we are in a relationship with someone, we know what buttons to push to get an emotional reaction. Sometimes pushing the hot button is done intentionally to punish or criticize the other person. Criticism can be used as a weapon to slowly chisel away at your spouse's character over time. Your criticism may have merit, but how and why you share it matters. The Bible says, "Do not let any unwholesome talk come out of your mouths, but only what is helpful for building others up according to their needs, that it may benefit those who listen" (Eph. 4:29). This is the compass that needs to guide your tough conversations with your spouse. The goal is to build them up and benefit them by speaking the truth in love with honor, respect, and empathy. Can you spot the difference between these two criticisms?

> A. All you do is play video games. You are so lazy; you never help with dinner.
> B. I know you love video games; however, I am feeling frustrated about them tonight because I am exhausted and could really use your help with dinner.

COLLABORATE INSTEAD OF ACCUSING

Collaboration leads you to ask questions, to be curious and seek understanding. However, when you make an accusation, you reveal that you've already reached the verdict that your spouse is guilty without hearing all the facts of the case or your spouse's perspective. Now, that doesn't seem fair, does it? Teammates work together toward a common goal. Tough conversations are not about proving who's guilty or innocent but about working as a team to tackle problems together. The Bible says, "Do nothing from selfish ambition or conceit, but in humility count others more significant than yourselves. Let each of you look not only to his own interests, but also to the interests of others" (Phil. 2:3–4 ESV).

STICK TO ONE ISSUE AT A TIME

Sometimes when couples talk about tough topics, they want to talk about everything all at once, including old fights or old issues. Like my (Tondra's) grandmother used to say to us as kids, "When I get you, I'm gonna get you for the old and the new." She was saying when we finally had to deal with the issues, she would bring up everything she had been holding on to from past times and the new things. If your spouse thinks you're going to bombard them with past problems, they will be more reluctant to have a conversation about the present problem. No wise person is going to walk into an ambush knowingly and willingly. To be productive when tackling tough conversations, keep diversions and rabbit trails to a minimum, focus on the end result, and don't rehash old fights or old issues. Be clear and concise with what you want to say.

RESPONDING IN THE RIGHT WAY

Another tip for tackling tough conversations is be sure to have the right response when your spouse becomes vulnerable in the conversation. We cannot express to you enough just how critical this piece of the puzzle is to a winning marriage game plan. When someone has exposed themselves in such a naked and defenseless way, they have put themselves in your hands for safety. With this comes the responsibility of having a response that fosters connection, understanding, and acceptance.

Having the right response begins with giving up the need to be right. Giving up the need to be right moves us from being self-focused to being other-focused. This will lead us to ask the right questions instead of trying to prove we have the right answer. We can then be put in the mindset to learn and understand instead of teaching, proving, or blaming. The Bible says, "If one gives an answer before he hears, it is his folly and shame" (Prov. 18:13 ESV). The goal of communication is to be understood, and to understand, you must hear and listen. As noted by Stephen Covey and others, "People don't care how much you know until they know how much you care."[13]

Seeking understanding instead of giving answers brings connection because it allows you to join your spouse where they are. Understanding your spouse is a huge gift to them. Loneliness is an epidemic in our culture today. Loneliness has nothing to do with proximity to people. You can be surrounded by millions of people and still feel lonely. You can be in a marriage and still feel lonely because loneliness stems from feeling that you are not understood, that no one gets you. Having the right response gives your spouse the gift of feeling like they are understood and not alone in whatever they are dealing with.

> *Having the right response begins with giving up the need to be right.*

One day George walked off his job and never went back. I cannot say it was out of the blue; he had been sharing how toxic the work environment was daily. During those days we needed every penny to live on. We had not discussed anything about his quitting his job, especially without his finding another job first. When he called me at work and told me he had quit on the spot, all sorts of emotions ran through my body all at one time. By the time I got home, I was angry. When I walked through the door and saw him, God would not allow any of the angry things I had rehearsed in my head on the drive home to come out of my mouth. George was able to speak first, and he was apologetic and did not make any excuse for quitting his job without having another one.

He was already aware of how his decision had impacted us and was beating himself up in his own head as well as trying to find a solution. That pause allowed me to listen and respond with compassion and understanding. I was able to comfort and support George at that moment. George later told me that in that moment all he desperately needed from me was understanding and the way I responded made him feel we were on the same team, and this let him know he could come to me in the future with tough issues. The right response was the thing that brought us into alignment with an issue that could have torn us apart.

You communicate understanding by acknowledging and validating what your spouse is saying and feeling. To acknowledge means you hear the words they are saying. Acknowledgment does not mean that you agree with them but that their point of view is important to you. Everyone has a right to their perspective, so honor their position even if you do not agree. Take it seriously and hear them out. Dean Rusk, the second-longest-serving US secretary of state, once said, "One of the best ways to persuade others is with your ears—by listening to them."[14]

After you acknowledge what your spouse is saying, then validate what they are feeling. Validation requires getting in touch with your spouse's emotions. We know we just lost 90 percent of the men, but hang in there with us. Validation is learning about your spouse's emotions and accepting their emotional experience even if it's different from yours. When you dismiss or reject your spouse by saying they are being too sensitive or overreacting or by telling them they should not feel what they are feeling, it is invalidating, which is the opposite of validation. Validation may look different for men and women. Typically, men need to process through logic to understand their feelings, while women need to process through their feelings to understand the logic. However, this could be different in your relationship. Just observe each other and figure out your specific dynamic. No matter how you process, your way is not the best or only way. Through our different ways, we help each other grow and become more balanced.

The more logical processor will desire to move past emotions quickly or, better yet, to skip that part. This may be because the logical processor may not know what to do or how to handle the emotion. Emotions may overwhelm or flood them, and they will do and say anything to get out of that moment, including shutting down or agreeing to move on even though they disagree. On the flip side, the emotional processor may want to linger in the emotional space, not really desiring to move to the logic, just letting the emotions be the end of the story.

The goal is to create space and allow each person to process the way they need to. To do this, each of you will need to tolerate the uncomfortable part of the conversation, the part that doesn't come naturally for you. As you continue to practice, your tolerance level will increase, and before you know it, the uncomfortable part will seem more and more comfortable.

You cannot have an effective marriage game plan without learning how to effectively tackle tough conversations together. As couples, knowing what to say, how to say it, when to say it, and how to respond to what's said will give you a framework for navigating these tough conversations. The Bible says, "Know this, my beloved brothers: let every person be quick to hear, slow to speak, slow to anger; for the anger of man does not produce the righteousness of God" (James 1:19–20

ESV). When you learn these skills, they will produce good things in your relationship, allowing you to reflect God's character in the way you love, honor, and respect each other.

> *You cannot have an effective marriage game plan without learning how to effectively tackle tough conversations together.*

Putting It into Practice

QUESTIONS

1. What impacted you most from this chapter, and why?

2. Which tip for tackling tough conversations is the most challenging for you personally, and why?

3. What are the hot topics in your relationship, and what makes them difficult to discuss?

4. What would make it easier to tackle tough conversations in your relationship?

5. What's one thing that you would implement to make you feel safer when it comes to tackling tough conversations? Why is it important to include this?

COUPLE'S ACTIVITY: CREATING A SAFE SPACE

Take a few moments to answer the following questions individually. Be honest! Next, take turns sharing your responses while utilizing the tips we discussed in this chapter. We've listed some samples of "acknowledging and validating" responses you can use to create a safe space when your spouse is sharing. Remember, avoiding or delaying tough conversations only makes things worse and compounds the tension, making it more difficult to have these conversations.

Here are some tips to help you find the right words:

- Write out what you want to say first.
- Start off positively.
- Take out negatively charged words.
- Collaborate instead of accusing.
- Stick to one issue at a time.

1. What was most challenging for you last year?

2. What concerns you the most in this season?

3. What do you need more of or less of in our relationship, and why?

FINDING THE RIGHT RESPONSES

Acknowledge

- This is not a time for problem-solving or solutions.
- You don't have to agree.
- Let your spouse know their perspective is important.

Validate

Learn and be curious about your spouse's emotions and experiences. Here are some sample responses to help you validate the speaker:

- Nod your head and make eye contact.
- "Tell me more" (show interest).
- "What was that like for you?"
- "How does that impact you?"
- "Yeah, I can see how that might make you feel _____."
- "What does that mean for you?"
- "One thing I appreciate about you is _____ [say a quality that builds their confidence in the situation]."
- "Oh no, I know how much that meant/means to you."
- "How did/does that make you feel?"
- Ask a curious question to gain more understanding.

- "I would be _____ [upset, nervous, sad, scared, disappointed, etc.] too!"
- "That must have been _____ [hard, upsetting, frightening, disappointing, etc.]."

PRAYER POINTS TO CONSIDER

ACTION ITEMS
(What steps, actions, or decisions do you need to make or take?)

TIME-OUT

For further insights and practical tips from this chapter, take a time-out and view our short bonus video, "Time-Out: Tips for Tackling Tough Conversations," using this link or QR code:

https://davidccook.org/access

Access code: GamePlan

Chapter 10

DEVELOPING YOUR MARRIAGE GAME PLAN

Some people want it to happen, some wish it would happen, others make it happen.
Michael Jordan

Achieving a successful marriage requires more than saying "I do" and hoping and praying that it will last for a lifetime. We strongly believe that for couples to win and be successful at staying together, they must know their marriage game plan—a set of strategies and actionable steps. A well-laid-out marriage game plan puts couples on the same page and keeps them going in the same direction. As we've shown, when couples are not on the same page, it causes them to lose sight of the big picture.

Now that you've finished the reading, watched the "Time-Out" videos, thoughtfully answered the questions, and worked through the activities from the "Putting It into Practice" section at the end of each chapter, you're ready to assemble your own marriage game plan! This chapter will become the catalyst to give you and your spouse your game plan for life with a clear strategy to grow and win together.

Just as athletes use a playbook to ensure they know their team's plays, plan of action, and strategy to win, you will have a familiar resource you've written and designed together. We've broken this chapter into five sections that will become the key building blocks of your marriage game plan as outlined in chapter 1:

Section 1: Define Your Win
Section 2: Set Your Goals
Section 3: Know Your Team
Section 4: Know Your Team's Opponents
Section 5: Design Your Plan of Action

Here's what you can expect in the first four sections:

- You'll have an opportunity to personalize your game plan by incorporating the answers from the questions and activities completed with your spouse at the end of each chapter. If you haven't finished the questions and activities, we encourage you to do so, as they are intended to assist you in tailoring your marriage game plan to your unique needs.
- You'll find time-tested marriage coaching tips to implement the insights and tools acquired from reading *The Marriage Game Plan*. Just as continually practicing enables elite athletes to succeed, consistently practicing these proven marriage coaching tips as a couple will enhance your success. Practice and exercise these tips throughout your marriage, making them part of your lifestyle rather than discarding them after finishing this resource.

Section 5 is where you can list all your action items from the end of each chapter. Once you've completed all the sections, you will have a marriage game plan to help you keep in mind the big picture of obtaining marital success.

SECTION 1: DEFINE YOUR WIN

The desire to win together in marriage is the foundation and beginning of clarity and agreement. Defining the win shows you what success looks like as an endgame picture. The success of a marriage is built on a couple's shared purpose, vision, mission, and value system.

YOUR MARRIAGE VISION STATEMENT

Insert your marriage vision statement (chapter 1, Couple's Activity) from page 28:

YOUR MARRIAGE MISSION STATEMENT

Insert your marriage mission statement (chapter 1, Couple's Activity) from page 30:

YOUR WEDDING VOW RENEWAL

Insert your wedding vows and covenants (chapter 2, Couple's Activity) from page 47. If they're too long for this space, please print a copy and attach them to your game plan. Continue to live out your wedding vows as a daily practice throughout your marriage. Have a specific time once a year to remember and reflect on what you've committed to on your journey together.

MARRIAGE COACHING TIPS FROM CHAPTERS 1 AND 2
Marriage Game Plan and Playbook

- Keep the end-goal picture at the forefront of your mind.
- Consistently communicate your needs and desires to your spouse.
- Be intentional about building a team of oneness and solidarity.
- Avoid assuming that your partner inherently understands your needs or expectations.
- Make it a habit to consistently express heartfelt gratitude and appreciation for your spouse.
- Strive to reflect God's image to each other and the community around you by daily practicing love, patience, forgiveness, and compassion.
- Embrace the concept of "we" rather than "me," and work together to build a strong and cohesive partnership.

SECTION 2: SET YOUR GOALS

Goal setting involves taking active steps to achieve your desired outcome of winning in your marriage. Clearly defining the win in your marriage, or how you envision a successful marriage, will then lead to setting clear goals and objectives as a couple to achieve your endgame picture. Couples win when there are clear indicators and benchmarks to measure their progress and success.

Insert your relationship goals (chapter 3, Couple's Activity) from page 64:

Insert your relationship declaration statements (chapter 3, Couple's Activity) from page 65:

Insert your marriage Scripture verses to stand on (chapter 3, Couple's Activity) from page 65:

MARRIAGE COACHING TIPS FROM CHAPTER 3
Winning the Home Game

- Your success as a couple is found in working together and establishing routines and habits that help you win your home game.
- Prioritize rest and recovery to help you execute at your optimal performance each day.
- Read God's playbook (the Bible) to help you maintain the right mindset and attitude to succeed at winning the home game.
- Maintain mental toughness through life's ups and downs to keep your perspective clear.
- Embrace the mindset that you can win against all odds as a team.

SECTION 3: KNOW YOUR TEAM

Knowing your team helps assess the team's differences, strengths, and growth areas.

CODE PHRASE

Insert your unique code phrase (chapter 4, Couple's Activity) from page 83:

Remember to employ your unique code phrase as a gentle reminder when you feel like you are enemies and tensions are rising. Despite disagreements, you are on the same team working toward common goals.

JOURNEY FOR LIFE KEY VERSE

Print and hang the Journey for Life Version of Ecclesiastes 4:9–10, 12, found on pages 83–84 (chapter 4, Couple's Activity).

Remember to make two copies and personalize the Scripture by inserting your spouse's name in the blanks. Place the Scripture passage in your home in an area that you tend to run to the most when times get rough, as a reminder that you're united in purpose, striving to support and uplift each other toward success and victory. Allow this Scripture to become a key verse over the course of your marriage journey.

MARRIAGE COACHING TIPS FROM CHAPTERS 4, 6, AND 7

We Are on the Same Team

- Always remember that you and your spouse are on the same team.
- Maintain a willingness to do whatever it takes for your marriage team to win.
- As Coach Jim Harbaugh, head coach of the Los Angeles Chargers, once said, "Being the guardian of victory is probably the number-one job you have. Making sure that the decisions you're making are complementary on all three phases. There's no offense. There's no defense. It's a we-fense."[1]
- Never forget—your spouse is not your enemy!
- Remember that marriage is a covenant, not a contract.
- Accept your spouse's differences and allow them to fill your gaps. (Refer to questions 2–3 from chapter 4, page 81.)
- Remember that selfishness can destroy a marriage.

Trusting Your Teammate

- Continue to practice and develop covenant communication skills to maintain honor and respect in your relationship. (Refer to the "Covenant Communication" activity from chapter 6, pages 126–28.)

- Make it a habit to discuss finances regularly, and seek out a financial adviser as needed.
- Make date nights a regular part of your weekly schedule to maintain closeness and connection.
- Prioritize times during the week to work on things you need to address as a couple (work zones). This will alleviate bringing up tough conversations at the wrong time.
- Agree on times during the week that are free to enjoy personal time and each other without fear of being blindsided by conversations that may spark tension (free zones).
- Maintain intimacy integrity to sustain the vulnerability needed for a healthy sex life.
- Dedicate yourself to nurturing a secure environment where trust can thrive by relinquishing any alternative plans or fallback options (no plan B).

Building Friendship

- Continue building and nurturing your friendship as the feeling of being in love comes and goes. (Refer to the "Connection Conversation" activity from chapter 7 on pages 143–44.)
- Prioritize Victory Mondays in your routine as a couple to celebrate both major and minor achievements.
- Schedule regular "team huddles" during the week to foster connection and unity.

SECTION 4: KNOW YOUR TEAM'S OPPONENTS

Couples must be able to identify key opponents (obstacles, enemies, patterns, mindsets) that stand in the way of their desired outcome in marriage. Where there is a strong desire to win, there will also be fierce opponents that will attempt to upend your marriage game plan.

Insert your rules of engagement (chapter 8, Couple's Activity) from page 162.

MARRIAGE COACHING TIPS FROM CHAPTERS 5, 8, AND 9
Teamwork in Conflict

- Make it a habit to navigate disagreements constructively. (Refer to the "Unity in Conflict" activities from chapter 8, pages 162–67.)
- Proactively recognize and address personal triggers to mitigate potential conflicts.
- Remember, every couple has obstacles they must overcome to be a winning team.
- Remember, it's "Happy spouse, happy house," not "Happy wife, happy life."

Facing and Overcoming Your Opponents

- Make it a habit to periodically explore and process how your past baggage might be showing up in your relationship. (Refer to the "Background Reflection" activity from chapter 5, pages 99–102.)
- Foster a mindset that emphasizes positive thoughts regarding your spouse and the relationship you share.
- Prevent bad seeds from taking root and leaving you with bitterness and resentment in your heart.
- Make it a habit to seek and grant forgiveness to live a life of freedom and peace.
- Be careful about what and how you think because your thoughts determine the quality of your life and relationships.

- Maintain a growth mindset, which allows you to embrace challenges and learn new things.
- Plant God's seed in your hearts together and separately through reading the Bible, listening to worship songs, and praying.

Tips for Tackling Tough Conversations

- Commit to have the right words and the right responses when addressing hot topics. (Refer to the "Creating a Safe Space" activity from chapter 9, pages 184–86.)
- Remember, ignoring unhealthy coping mechanisms prevents you from adapting and adjusting to what's needed for healthy communication.
- Commit to seek out professional help to address unhealthy coping behaviors.

SECTION 5: DESIGN YOUR PLAN OF ACTION

List each action item that you have written as individuals and as a couple at the end of each chapter. You may also find it helpful to list any additional steps, decisions, or plans that you have discussed or desire to implement in your marriage game plan.

Chapter 1

Chapter 2

Chapter 3

Chapter 4

Chapter 5

Chapter 6

Chapter 7

Chapter 8

Chapter 9

CONCLUSION

Congratulations on completing your personalized marriage game plan! Through the hard work you've invested here, you've crafted a clear strategy for mutual growth and success. Together, you've defined your goals, set clear objectives, and identified your team's unique strengths, differences, and areas for growth. You've also acknowledged key challenges in your relationship and designed a proactive plan of action to address them. With your marriage game plan in hand, you and your spouse now have a clear path to pursue the marriage of your dreams.

Unlike most marriage books that conclude after you read and answer a few questions, *The Marriage Game Plan* is designed to be a continuous resource for you to revisit and expand upon as your relationship evolves over time. Your journey does not end with completing this book; rather, this book serves as a launching point for the future of your relationship. Your completed marriage game plan is intended to be an ongoing resource and tool to return to throughout your marriage, ensuring you remain on the same page, going in the same direction and growing as a couple.

Now that you've finished this book and formulated your marriage game plan, we encourage you both to:

- Put your game plan into action and follow through with what you've agreed upon.
- Regularly revisit the Couple's Activities to refine your skills.
- Adapt and adjust your strategy as circumstances change.

- Seek professional support when necessary.
- Celebrate your achievements and milestones together.
- Engage with one of *The Marriage Game Plan*'s online coaching groups for additional support.
- Subscribe to *The Marriage Game Plan* podcast for additional resources and insightful tips.

The secret to a great marriage is two people working hard to make it work. Now that you have your personal marriage game plan, it's your turn to continue to work hard at implementing and executing your game plan to build a loving, lifelong marriage. God bless you on your marriage journey.

SMALL GROUP GUIDE

Welcome to *The Marriage Game Plan* small group guide! We hope you've enjoyed working through the book together and that you'll also enjoy discussion time with friends. Each of the five sessions in this guide covers two chapters from the book. In discussing these additional questions, you can encourage others in their marriages by sharing how *The Marriage Game Plan* encouraged you!

FOR THE LEADER

Thank you for deciding to guide your small group through this book. This will be a time of growth for all involved, and your willingness to share and facilitate discussion will provide a space for that growth.

In general, we recommend the following order for your meeting times:

1. Open with mingling and fellowship, so group members can catch up and connect.
2. Pray to set the tone.

3. Discuss the chapters using the questions in this guide.
4. Close with prayer requests, prayer, and any follow-up.

This flow can be tailored to each individual group. Also keep in mind that, depending on whether the group is mainly women, men, or couples, some of the questions may feel too personal to discuss. Use your discretion and familiarity with the group to decide which questions to ask and which to save for another setting. If your group is one that seems willing to go deep and continue the discussion longer, be bold and include the **Share Deeper Question (SDQ)** and consider bringing in some of the questions at the end of each chapter.

Discuss with the group the importance of working on their marriage game plan in Chapter 10 to get the most out of the book and group experience. The section at the end of each chapter, "Putting It into Practice," guides couples in crafting their marriage game plan. Chapter 10 serves couples as an ongoing strategy they can revisit, adapt, and adjust over the lifetime of their marriage.

As a small group facilitator, please don't feel pressure to be a marriage expert or know how to answer all questions on marriage and relationships. If couples need a higher level of care and support, feel free to direct them to engage with one of *The Marriage Game Plan* online coaching groups or one-on-one private relationship coaching through the Gregorys' website, https://journeyforlifenow.org.

Take the lead in providing a means for your group to connect outside of your regular meeting times. Provide a sign-up sheet for people to provide their emails or cell phone numbers if they would like to opt into group communications. This will enable your members to form relationships and continue them—even after the study concludes.

Finally, don't forget to pray, not just during your group time, but in between sessions. Nothing moves hearts like prayer, so be sure to pray for the members of your group on a regular basis.

For more vision and direction on leading your small group, please see our short video, "Message for Small Group Leaders," accessed through this link or QR code: https://davidccook.org/access. Access code: GamePlan

FOR THE PARTICIPANTS
SESSION 1: CHAPTERS 1 & 2

1. What from the two chapters stood out to you most?

2. In general, what do you see as the biggest benefit of having a marriage game plan, and why?

3. What are you most excited about incorporating into your marriage game plan?

4. Read the explanations for the bond between a husband and wife on pages 35–39. Which one most resonated with you? Why?

SDQ: How could your marriage most benefit from a game plan?

SESSION 2: CHAPTERS 3 & 4

1. What from the two chapters stood out to you most?

2. What is one method of dealing with stress as a team you've decided on that may help others in the group?

3. How does knowing that God created marriage change the way you view the institution of marriage?

4. What are some tactics that our true Enemy, the Devil, commonly uses to undermine marriages in our culture today?

5. What is the difference between a contract and a covenant?

SDQ: How has the Enemy been trying to undermine your marriage?

SESSION 3: CHAPTERS 5 & 6

1. What from the two chapters stood out to you most?

2. How would you define an "opponent" to a healthy marriage?

3. What are some good seeds to plant in a marriage? What are some bad seeds?

4. What are some ways to encourage a growth mindset in yourself and your marriage?

5. What strategies are helpful in fostering effective communication?

SDQ: Who, or what, has been an opponent in your marriage? How did you face and overcome the opponent together?

SESSION 4: CHAPTERS 7 & 8

1. What from the two chapters stood out to you most?

2. Is there a recent win in your marriage that you feel comfortable sharing? How can you celebrate that win?

3. Which of the "Seven C's of Strengthening Friendship" can you implement in your marriage this week?

4. How would you describe a unified couple?

5. What Scripture passages speak to resolving conflict and building unity?

SDQ: What is your strongest unified trait as a couple?

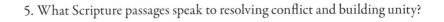

Note: To be prepared for our next session, be sure you have completed your marriage game plan in chapter 10.

SESSION 5: CHAPTERS 9 & 10 PLUS WRAP-UP

1. What are some harmful ways to handle tough conversations? What are some helpful ways?

2. How can applying these helpful ways enhance conflict-resolution skills?

3. How does having a marriage game plan empower you and your spouse to build your marriage?

SDQ: How has this book's content and this group most encouraged you?

ACKNOWLEDGMENTS

We are deeply grateful for the many individuals who have played a role in bringing *The Marriage Game Plan* to life.

First and foremost, we thank God for His guidance, wisdom, and grace in our lives and our journey for life. Without His hand in our marriage, this book would not exist. Our hope is that every couple who reads this will feel His presence in their relationship as they build their own marriage game plan.

To our dear family and friends: Thank you for your unwavering support, encouragement, and love throughout this process. You've been our rock, especially during the long hours and many sacrifices that went into writing this book.

A special thanks to Pastor Rick Warren for writing the foreword and believing in the vision behind this work. Your influence on our lives and ministry has been profound, and we are honored to call you pastor and friend.

To Coach Anthony Lynn, Coach Leslie Frazier, and Coach George Stewart: Thank you for your heartfelt endorsements and for championing the importance of healthy marriages within the sports world. Your voices have brought this book to new heights, and we are so grateful for your friendship.

To our Journey for Life board: Thank you for standing with us in our mission to equip and educate couples. Your support and shared passion for strengthening marriages has been invaluable, and this work would not be possible without your dedication.

To our mentors: Your wisdom, guidance, and example have deeply influenced our lives and this book. Thank you for pouring into us, teaching us, and inspiring us to be better leaders and servants in the world of marriage and family.

To all the churches that believed in us and invited us to share our strategies and talks at your churches, getaways, and retreats: Thank you for opening your doors and hearts to us. Your belief in our mission has been a tremendous encouragement, and we are grateful to have partnered with you.

To Pastors Clayton and Ashlee Hurst, marriage pastors at Lakewood Church: Thank you for championing us and believing in our vision, dream, abilities, and calling. Your unwavering support has been a source of strength, and we are deeply grateful for your friendship and encouragement.

To the Los Angeles Chargers: Thank you for allowing us to walk alongside the team, corporate staff, and their families. Your commitment to fostering strong marriages and families has made a lasting impact, and we are honored to be a part of your community.

To the NFL players, coaches, and families we've had the privilege to serve over the years: Thank you for trusting us to walk with you through the ups and downs of life and marriage.

To Tom Dean, our literary agent: Thank you for your tireless efforts, guidance, and belief in this project. You have been instrumental in bringing this book into the hands of readers.

A special thanks to our publisher, David C Cook, for your partnership and commitment to our message. Your belief in the importance of strong, faith-based marriages has made this journey all the more meaningful.

To all the couples who are still fighting to make your marriage work: You inspire us every day. Your resilience, determination, and love are a testament to the power of faith and commitment. We honor you and hope this book equips you to keep thriving.

And finally, to every couple who is reading this book: Thank you for taking the time to invest in your marriage. Our prayer is that you find hope, strength, and practical wisdom to build a marriage that not only endures but thrives.

With love and gratitude,
George and Tondra Gregory

NOTES

CHAPTER 1: THE IMPORTANCE OF A GAME PLAN

1. "Lookin' for Love," on Johnny Lee, *Lookin' for Love*, Elektra Entertainment, 1980.

2. "Divorce Rates in the World: Divorce Rates by Country," Divorce.com, updated July 15, 2024, https://divorce.com/blog/divorce-rates-in-the-world.

3. "51+ Divorce Statistics in the U.S., Including Divorce Rate, Race, and Marriage Length," Divorce.com, updated July 15, 2024, https://divorce.com/blog/divorce-statistics.

4. "Divorce Rates in the World."

5. Christy Bieber, "Revealing Divorce Statistics in 2025," *Forbes*, updated November 20, 2024, www.forbes.com/advisor/legal/divorce/divorce-statistics.

6. Bieber, "Revealing Divorce Statistics."

7. Bieber, "Revealing Divorce Statistics."

8. Bieber, "Revealing Divorce Statistics."

9. David Lariviere, "Divorce, Not Domestic Violence, Is Biggest Issue at Home for Professional Athletes," *Forbes*, updated August 15, 2014, www.forbes.com/sites/davidlariviere/2014/08/15/divorce-not-domestic-violence-is-biggest-issue-at-home-for-professional-athletes.

10. "Divorce Statistics in the U.S. and Irvine, California," Wilkinson & Finkbeiner, accessed April 3, 2024, www.orangecountydivorce.com/divorce-statistics-in-the-u-s-and-irvine-california.

CHAPTER 2: THE PLAYBOOK ON MARRIAGE

1. "Strong's G4801—syzeugnymi," Blue Letter Bible, accessed November 7, 2024, www.blueletterbible.org/lexicon/g4801/nkjv/tr/0-1.

2. See "Strong's H5048—neged," Blue Letter Bible, accessed November 7, 2024, www.blueletterbible.org/lexicon/h5048/kjv/wlc/0-1; Kat Armas, "What Does 'Helper' Really Mean?," July 25, 2018, https://katarmas.com/blog/2018/8/3/what-does-helper-really-mean.

CHAPTER 3: WINNING THE HOME GAME

1. Maurizio R., "Mr. and Mrs. Smith—Final Scene," YouTube, August 16, 2009, www.youtube.com/watch?v=zIxGhLILsNs&ab_channel=MaurizioR.

2. A S, "Gladiator. The Scene # 'If We Stay Together, We Survive,'" YouTube, June 17, 2020, www.youtube.com/watch?v=4W-AZzxytZs.

3. Movieclips, "The Karate Kid (1984)—Wax On, Wax Off Scene," YouTube, September 6, 2022, www.youtube.com/watch?v=-P11Bcpyw4g.

4. Charles R. Swindoll, *Life Is 10% What Happens to You and 90% How You React* (Nashville, TN: Nelson Books, 2023), 183.

5. Associated Press, "Rivers Rallies Chargers Past Steelers 33–30," ESPN, updated December 3, 2018, www.espn.com/nfl/recap/_/gameId/401030951.

6. Jeff Miller, "Anthony Lynn Hopes the 2019 Chargers Can Be as Resilient and as Focused as 2018 Team," *Los Angeles Times*, August 15, 2019, www.latimes.com/sports/chargers/story/2019-08-15/anthony-lynn-resilient-chargers.

7. "What's a Personal Tagline, and Why You Need One Now!," PlanPlus Online, accessed March 29, 2024, www.planplusonline.com/whats-a-personal-tagline.

8. Julia Kay, "10 SMART Goal Examples: A Guide to Setting and Achieving Your Goals," BetterUp, February 10, 2025, www.betterup.com/blog/smart-goals-examples.

CHAPTER 4: WE ARE ON THE SAME TEAM

1. Prime Sports Media (@primesportsmedia06), "Deion Sanders Says, Colorado Will Win NOW," TikTok, July 9, 2023, www.tiktok.com/@primesportsmedia06/video/7253912669814590763?_r=1&_t=8kmvv029jn0.

2. Buffalo Archives Now, "Bills vs. Oilers Comeback Game—NFL PRIMETIME COVERAGE," YouTube, accessed April 10, 2022, www.youtube.com/watch?v=iZWgd4Bh39I; Chad Michael Murray, "1992—Oilers vs. Bills: AFC Wild Card—'the Comeback,'" NFL.com, accessed April 30, 2024, www.nfl.com/100/originals/100-greatest/games-7.

3. Sarah Calise, "A Foothold on History," National Baseball Hall of Fame, accessed May 30, 2024, https://baseballhall.org/discover-more/stories/short-stops/foothold-on-history.

4. "Super Bowl LI: New England 34, Atlanta 28 OT," New England Patriots, accessed April 30, 2024, www.patriots.com/press-room/super-bowl-li.

5. "Battier, Williams Come Alive Late to Rescue Duke," ESPN, January 27, 2001, www.espn.com/ncb/2001/20010127/recap/daumaj.html.

6. Basket Ball, "The Greatest Comeback in NBA History, 36 Points Deficit, Utah Jazz against Denver Nuggets 1996," YouTube, January 11, 2021, www.youtube.com/watch?v=lDQ92kCCbQc.

7. "Jim Harbaugh on Coaching: 'Theres No Offense. There's No Defense. There's a We-fense,'" Michigan Insider, September 4, 2023, www.youtube.com/watch?v=Iu-soyP1RkM.

8. Charles Clay Doyle, Wolfgang Mieder, and Fred R. Shapiro, comps., *The Dictionary of Modern Proverbs* (New Haven, CT: Yale University Press, 2012), 229–30.

9. Jromero1982, "Rocky 'She Fills Gaps,'" YouTube, December 1, 2010, www.youtube.com/watch?v=tcqos-b3jDo.

10. NinjAthlete, "It's not what you're capable of, it's what you're willing to do," TikTok, September 20, 2023, www.tiktok.com/@ninjathlete/video/7280857786328649002.

CHAPTER 5: FACING AND OVERCOMING YOUR OPPONENTS

1. Life Innovations, Inc., *Workbook for Couples* (Minneapolis, MN: Prepare/Enrich, 2017), 15.

2. Nathan Collins, "Pathways: From the Eye to the Brain," *Stanford Medicine*, August 21, 2017, https://stanmed.stanford.edu/carla-shatz-vision-brain.

3. Ruth A. Lanius, Braeden A. Terpou, and Margaret C. McKinnon, "The Sense of Self in the Aftermath of Trauma: Lessons from the Default Mode Network in Posttraumatic Stress Disorder," *European Journal of Psychotraumatology* 11, no. 1 (2020), www.ncbi.nlm.nih.gov/pmc/articles/PMC7594748.

4. John D. Kelly IV, "Your Best Life: Managing Negative Thoughts—the Choice Is Yours," *Clinical Orthopaedics and Related Research,* 477, no. 2 (2019): 1291–93, www.ncbi.nlm.nih.gov/pmc/articles/PMC6554130.

5. Monica Vermani, "Why Our Negative Thoughts Are So Powerful," *Psychology Today*, September 25, 2023, www.psychologytoday.com/us/blog/a-deeper-wellness/202309/why-our-negative-thoughts-are-so-powerful.

6. Kyle Benson, "The Magic Relationship Ratio, according to Science," The Gottman Institute, updated September 18, 2024, www.gottman.com/blog/the-magic-relationship-ratio-according-science.

7. John M. Gottman and Nan Silver, *The Seven Principles for Making Marriage Work* (New York: Three Rivers Press, 1999), 61–72.

8. David T. Neal, Wendy Wood, Mengju Wu, and David Kurlander, "The Pull of the Past: When Do Habits Persist despite Conflict with Motives?," *Personality and Social Psychology Bulletin* 37, no. 11 (November 2011): 1428–37, https://journals.sagepub.com/doi/10.1177/0146167211419863.

9. Gina Ryder, "What Is Neuroplasticity?," PsychCentral, November 12, 2021, https://psychcentral.com/health/what-is-neuroplasticity.

10. Jennifer Smith, "Growth Mindset vs Fixed Mindset: How What You Think Affects What You Achieve," Mindset Health, September 25, 2020, www.mindsethealth.com/matter/growth-vs-fixed-mindset.

CHAPTER 6: TRUSTING YOUR TEAMMATE

1. Seth Meyers, "How Financial Problems and Stress Cause Divorce," *Psychology Today*, December 6, 2012, www.psychologytoday.com/us/blog/insight-is-2020/201212/how-financial-problems-stress-cause-divorce.

2. "Happy Couples: How to Avoid Money Arguments," American Psychological Association, 2015, www.apa.org/topics/money/conflict.

3. John M. Gottman and Nan Silver, *The Seven Principles for Making Marriage Work* (New York: Three Rivers Press, 1999), 25–26.

CHAPTER 7: VICTORY MONDAYS

1. Sara B. Algoe, Shelly L. Gable, and Natalya C. Maisel, "It's the Little Things: Everyday Gratitude as a Booster Shot for Romantic Relationships," *Personal Relationships* 17 (2010): 217–33, https://greatergood.berkeley.edu/images/uploads/Algoe-Gable-Maisel-2010-Its-the-little-things.pdf.

2. "After the Love Has Gone," on Earth, Wind & Fire, *I Am*, ARC/Columbia, 1979.

3. Philip Furia, "'Ac-Cent-Tchu-Ate the Positive'—Johnny Mercer (1944)," Library of Congress, accessed August 26, 2024, www.loc.gov/static/programs/national-recording-preservation-board/documents/AcCentTchuAteThePositive.pdf.

4. Whitney Johnson, "Celebrate to Win," *Harvard Business Review*, January 26, 2022, https://hbr.org/2022/01/celebrate-to-win.

CHAPTER 8: TEAMWORK IN CONFLICT

1. Krishna Kripalani, comp. and ed., *All Men Are Brothers* (Ahmedabad, India: Navajivan, 1960), 217.

CHAPTER 9: TIPS FOR TACKLING TOUGH CONVERSATIONS

1. Jennifer Caspari, "Embracing Vulnerability," *Psychology Today*, May 7, 2023, www.psychologytoday.com/us/blog/living-well-when-your-body-doesnt-cooperate/202305/embracing-vulnerability.

2. Arlin Cuncic, "What Is Maladaptive Behavior?," Verywell Mind, updated September 4, 2023, www.verywellmind.com/what-is-the-meaning-of-maladaptive-3024600.

3. Anna Katharina Schaffner, "10 Most Common Unhealthy Coping Mechanisms: A List," PositivePsychology.com, updated December 20, 2024, https://positivepsychology.com/unhealthy-coping-mechanisms.

4. Sanjana Gupta, "Deflection as a Defense Mechanism: Learn Why People Deflect and How to Deal with People Who Do It," Verywell Mind, February 28, 2023, www.verywellmind.com/deflection-as-a-defense-mechanism-7152445.

5. Charlie Huntington, "People Pleasing: Definition, Quotes, and Psychology," Berkeley Well-Being Institute, accessed August 26, 2024, www.berkeleywellbeing.com/people-pleasing.

6. Ashley Olivine, "Signs of Passive-Aggressive Behavior," Verywell Health, updated December 10, 2024, www.verywellhealth.com/addressing-passive-aggressive-behavior-5217046.

7. Kendra Cherry, "Aggression Explained: What It Is and How to Recognize It," Verywell Mind, January 8, 2025, www.verywellmind.com/what-is-aggression-2794818.

8. Schaffner, "10 Most Common Unhealthy Coping Mechanisms."

9. Schaffner, "10 Most Common Unhealthy Coping Mechanisms."

10. Kyle Benson, "The Magic Relationship Ratio, according to Science," The Gottman Institute, updated September 18, 2024, www.gottman.com/blog/the-magic-relationship-ratio-according-science.

11. Ben Martin, "Fight or Flight," PsychCentral, May 17, 2016, https://psychcentral.com/lib/fight-or-flight.

12. John M. Gottman and Nan Silver, *The Seven Principles for Making Marriage Work* (New York: Three Rivers Press, 1999), 27, 40, 161.

13. Stephen R. Covey, *The 7 Habits of Highly Effective People* (New York: Free Press, 2004), 331.

14. "Listening with Understanding and Empathy," Institute for Habits of the Mind, accessed March 30, 2024, www.habitsofmindinstitute.org/resources/hom-quotes/3-listening-understanding-empathy.

CHAPTER 10: DEVELOPING YOUR MARRIAGE GAME PLAN

1. "Jim Harbaugh on Coaching: 'Theres No Offense. There's No Defense. There's a We-fense,'" Michigan Insider, September 4, 2023, www.youtube.com/watch?v=Iu-soyP1RkM.

HOST *The Marriage* GAME PLAN
Couples Event at Your Church!

Bring couples together for a powerful kickoff event that launches a 10-week journey through *The Marriage Game Plan* workbook.

This is a meaningful opportunity to inspire and equip couples in your congregation to invest in their relationship. By walking through the workbook together, they'll gain practical tools to strengthen their marriage and build a foundation for lifelong love and fulfillment.

Everything you need to host is included!
Download the FREE *Marriage Game Plan Church Event Kit* by clicking the QR code below to access the link, and get started today.

Helping Couples Win the *Home* Game.

Journey for Life's mission is to educate and equip couples on their journey to have successful relationships and marriages through speaking, teaching, and coaching.

Coaching you on the road towards marital *bliss!*

Speaking Engagements
George and Tondra have a unique and dynamic speaking duo style that leaves audiences with strategic game plans and tangible takeaways which produce results. Book the Gregory's for conferences, retreats, or events.

Relationship Coaching
For more than twenty years George and Tondra have been relationship coaches to thousands of couples around the world and in professional sports including the NFL.

Through Journey for Life's relationship coaching program individuals, couples, or groups will:

- Acquire a clear strategy and game plan to navigate personal relationships
- Receive countless insights infused with practical applications to strengthen and improve your relationship

Sign up for online relationship coaching or book the Gregory's to speak at **journeyforlifenow.org** or **info@journeyforlifenow.org**

JOIN US.
SPREAD THE GOSPEL.
CHANGE THE WORLD.

We believe in equipping the local church with Christ-centered resources that empower believers, even in the most challenging places on earth.

We trust that God is *always* at work, in the power of Jesus and the presence of the Holy Spirit, inviting people into relationship with Him.

We are committed to spreading the gospel throughout the world—across villages, cities, and nations. We trust that the Word of God will transform lives and communities by bringing light to the darkness.

As a global ministry with a 150-year legacy, David C Cook is dedicated to this mission. Each time you purchase a resource or donate, you're supporting a ministry—helping spread the gospel, disciple believers, and raise up leaders in some of the world's most underserved regions.

Your support fuels this mission.
Your partnership sends the gospel where it's needed most.

Discover more. Be the difference.
Visit DavidCCook.org/Donate